A-2 ENGLISH B

ESSENTIAL VOCABULARY AND PRACTICE ACTIVITIES
ORGANIZED BY TOPIC FOR IB DIPLOMA

English B

MANUEL ACOSTA G
SILVANA KUSKUNOV

Elemi
INTERNATIONAL SCHOOLS PUBLISHER

Published by Elemi International Schools Publisher Ltd

Authors: Manuel Acosta G, Silvana Kuskunov

Series Editor: Mary James

Specialist Editor: Jennifer Peek

The author and publisher would like to acknowledge the very valuable input of Elisabet Aleu who reviewed and commented on the manuscript. Elisabet is an experienced educator and examiner of the IB Diploma.

First published 2021

10 9 8 7 6 5 4 3 2 1

A catalogue record of this title is available from the British Library
British Library Cataloguing in Publication Data

ISBN 978-1-9164131-9-1

Page layout/design by EMC Design Ltd
Cover design by Jayne Martin-Kaye

Contents

	Page
Introduction	4
1 Identities	5
A Lifestyles	5
B Health and wellbeing	8
C Beliefs and values	11
D Subcultures	14
E Language and identity	17
2 Experiences	20
A Leisure activities	20
B Holidays and travel	22
C Life stories	24
D Rites of passage	27
E Customs and traditions	29
F Migration	31
3 Human ingenuity	33
A Entertainment	33
B Artistic expression	35
C Communication and media	37
D Technology	42
E Scientific innovation	45
4 Social organization	48
A Social relationships	48
B Community	51
C Social engagement	53
D Education	56
E The working world	59
F Law and order	62
5 Sharing the planet	65
A The environment	65
B Human rights	68
C Peace and conflict	71
D Equality	75
E Globalization	78
F Ethics	81
G Urban and rural environment	84
6 Language for the oral assessment	87
A Describing a photo or image (SL)	87
B Describing a literary extract (HL)	90
7 A guide to text types	92

Studying English B at IB Diploma

The IB English B Diploma programme is a rigorous and challenging language acquisition course which helps develop your linguistic skills as well as your inter-cultural understanding.

How this resource can help you

Studying English B as part of the IB Diploma programme involves a substantial amount of time for independent study and you may need additional support from your teacher, friends, or other resources. Of course, your teacher and friends may not always be available, particularly when it comes to acquiring, learning, and using a broad range of language and vocabulary across a variety of different topics.

This book aims to help you by providing a core of vocabulary and language organized by the themes and topics you will be studying as part of your IB Diploma.

- There are five broad themes (sections 1–5 in this book). Each theme has been divided into topics, and each topic is then further divided into sub-topics. These are organized along the following lines:
  - individual words together with useful verbs and verb collocations (ie words which are often used in combination). Note that these verbs are listed in the infinitive form.
  - idiomatic language and phrases on the topic which you are likely to meet and need as part of your studies.
- Each sub-topic also includes valuable vocabulary practice activities (eg on nuance and shades of meaning) to help you build your vocabulary in both spoken and written English. These activities also make suggestions for articles and podcasts for further reading and listening.
- Section 6 provides you with more generic language to help with the preparation of your individual oral assessment. At SL, you will engage in a conversation with your teacher which includes you describing a visual stimulus, like a photo. HL students will take part in a conversation related to an extract taken from one of the literary works studied as part of the course.
- Section 7 provides you with a guide to different text types, summarizing the features and style of language you will typically find when working with different texts in English.
- Generally, the language you are given in this resource is in standard register. Words and phrases which reflect more idiomatic language are described as such.
- Note this is not a comprehensive list of topical language and you are encouraged to acquire a broad range of vocabulary. If your teacher gives you additional words, or through your own reading you come across suitable language, you might choose to write it into this book, so it becomes more like a personal vocabulary book for you.
- When studying the language for each section in this book, remember that there may be useful and relevant vocabulary in another section. By cross referring between the different sections, you may find opportunities to blend the language from different themes and sub-topics. This is another way in which you can personalize the language for your own needs.

We wish you the best on your learning journey and, of course, the greatest success in your exams!

Manuel, Silvana, and the team at Elemi

Identities

A Lifestyles

vegan (noun/adj)
An individual who does not consume food that comes from animals and mostly does not use products derived from animals.
My choice to become a vegan has not been made on a whim, I carefully studied the effects of such a diet and I am trying to supplement myself accordingly.

strength (noun), **to strengthen** (verb)
The quality of having great power or potency; being able to resist great force.
Emotional strength can help us handle difficult situations.

leisure (noun/adj)
Free time when you can relax.
During next week's day off, I'll use my leisure time to catch up on my reading.

stress (noun/verb), **stressful** (adj)
A state of high tension. Feeling under pressure, or that it's hard to cope.
As if feeling this inordinate amount of stress wasn't enough, now they've moved the deadline to tomorrow!

hobby (hobbies) (noun)
Enjoyable activities done during leisure time.
Whenever I'm free or have some free time, I pursue my hobbies, such as finger painting and pottery.

poor nutrition (phrase) *or* **malnourishment** (noun)
Unhealthy, bad, or poor food that could be detrimental to an individual's health.
You can credit his stress to poor nutrition to some extent, since bad eating habits can sometimes have an unwanted effect on the mind.

health (noun), **healthy** (adj)
An absence of illness. An individual's physical or mental condition.
His health deteriorated after the accident; he might not walk again without aid, and he finds exercise difficult.

wellness (noun)
A state of proper care achieved through exercise and good nourishment.
His focus on improving his physical wellness has shown us the extent of his determination to live an active and healthier lifestyle.

gregarious (adj), **gregariousness** (noun)
An individual who enjoys the company of others.
A gregarious man, he always enjoyed hanging around and meeting new people.

indoor (adj), **indoors** (adv)/ **outdoor** (adj), **outdoors** (adv)
Inside or outside a building or place.
We decided to stay indoors during the thunderstorm, our house is safer than the park.
They place the hounds in the outdoor area of the compound so they can secure the perimeter.

sybarite (noun)
An individual fond of luxury and over-indulgence.
They consider the man from the mansion a committed sybarite who organizes very extravagant parties.

nomad (noun)
Individuals who tend to move recurrently, never settling in one place. Has a tendency to constantly move without settling permanently.
As nomads, they valued travelling through lands where their animals could graze and have their needs tended to.

self-absorbed (adj)
Mostly focused on one's own self and condition.
Self-absorbed people can be perceived as introverted who only care about themselves.

workaholic (noun)
Someone who is intently focused on or addicted to working to the detriment of any other activity.
As a workaholic, he's been neglecting his family in favour of working long hours every day.

bohemian (noun/adj)
Carefree and unburdened by responsibility or limitations. Non-conventional and unorthodox.
He came to the party breaking the dress-code, his unique outfit shows what a bohemian he is.

hedonism (noun)
Indulgence and pursuit of pleasure and satisfaction.
College students sometimes tend to indulge in hedonism as they explore their place in the social order.

party animal (noun)
Someone who enthusiastically enjoys parties and social gatherings.
Your cousin is a party animal, he kept partying until five o'clock in the morning!

recluse (noun), **reclusive** (adj)
Someone who prefers to stay indoors and keep to themself, with a tendency to avoid outside influence.
When I'm studying hard for my exams, I can become a recluse, avoiding contact even with my friends.

middle class (noun), **middle-class** (adj)
Median to high-income social position. Not particularly wealthy, but with enough money to cover most needs.
Middle-class families try to ensure their children get a good education.

subsistence (noun/adj)
A state where you just have what you need to survive.
In difficult times, subsistence farming has become a trend throughout the lowlands.

sedentary (adj)
A state of infrequent physical exertion or exercise; resting and being seated.
Office workers are prone to leading a sedentary way of life, especially if they work long hours.

longevity (noun)
A state of existing for an extended period in time.
Her longevity is attributed to her healthy lifestyle and proper diet.

conventional (adj)
Ordinary. Not deviating from the norm. Expected by most.
Students are expected to perform their activities in a conventional manner, despite having to work from home.

intake (noun)
The amount you take in, consume, eat, drink something. This could be food, air, etc.
Your vitamin intake has dropped this month, that's probably why you're so distracted during class.

edgy (adj)
1 To describe an individual who is tense, nervous, or irritable.
One would say that his edgy personality is what constantly gets him into trouble, patience is a virtue he hasn't mastered.

2 (informal) Unconventional, innovative.
One would say that his edgy style and tastes really define him.

austere (adj)
A way of life without many luxuries.
As a religious woman, she had very austere living conditions at the convent.

reflective (adj)
The quality of being capable of deep thought regarding a particular topic.
As a deeply reflective individual, you can better understand the events that take place around you.

sustainable (adj), **sustainability** (noun)
A way of describing a proper use of the world's natural resources to avoid damaging the environment.
I do whatever I can to eat a plant-based diet and contribute towards a more sustainable society.

balance (noun/verb), **balanced** (adj)
Equilibrium between elements, feelings, conditions, etc.
Since the global pandemic, we can see more and more the benefits of a work-life balance.

1 **Use your own words to paraphrase these idioms.**

   i)   Always look on the bright side of life.

   ii) The best things in life are free.

   iii) If life gives you lemons make lemonade.

2 **Match the situation (on the left) to the correct phrase (on the right).**

   i)   In the pandemic, doctors are putting their lives on the line.   to be full of/bursting with

   ii) How are you doing? Alive and kicking?   to be at risk

   iii) The school is teeming with students again.   to be fine

   iv) I am having the time of my life on this trip.   that is the way it is

   v)   This IB course is a real challenge. That's life!   the best moment/a memorable time

3 **Find the opposite meanings (or antonyms) of these words. You may use the vocabulary list above. (The first one has been done for you.)**

conservative	reserved	thoughtful	sporty	outgoing	idle
unconventional					

4 **Here are some newspaper headlines or quotes. Read, share, and discuss.**

   "#TUESDAYMOTIVATION: THE BEST IS YOUR NORMAL. DON'T SETTLE FOR LESS – ADEYEMI"
   Allure Vanguard, 19th January 2021

   "How this Pāpāmoa father became king of the sandcastle"
   Cari Johnson, *This NZ Life*, published 2020

B Health and wellbeing

lifestyle (noun)
A way of living adherent to various considerations.
One needs to consume less junk food in order to lead a healthier lifestyle.

healthcare (noun)
Organized medical care for individuals in need.
Providing healthcare to refugees and those in need should always be paramount.

welfare (noun)
State of happiness and good physical and mental health. Might also describe aid given by the government or an organization to those in need.
Eating vegetables and getting plenty of sleep go a long way to improving your general welfare.

fit (adj), **fitness** (noun)
Healthy in good physical condition. Proper quality, in a good state.
No matter how old he is, he constantly trains to stay fit and retain peak fitness.

disease (noun), **diseased** (adj)
Lack of good health, an abnormal detrimental state of illness.
After smoking so much, he seems to be suffering from a chronic respiratory disease.

ache (noun/verb)
A continuous enduring dull pain in a part of your body.
Aches and pains are a natural part of an intense workout session.

pain (noun/verb)
Discomfort due to an injury or illness.
Chemotherapy can generate a lot of pain for the patient, but it's a necessary treatment to combat cancer.

complexion (noun)
The appearance, colouring, and texture of an individual's skin.
He had a very fair complexion despite working in the mines for many years.

resilience (*or* **resiliency**) (noun), **resilient** (adj)
The ability to carry on despite hardship and face setbacks calmly.
After her father's passing, her resilience helped her finish her studies despite her grief.

self-esteem (noun)
How you feel about yourself. For those who we describe as having (good) self-esteem, we are describing them as confident and assured. The opposite where someone has low (or poor) self-esteem refers to them lacking self-respect or feeling they are not good enough.
Her self-esteem took a blow when she realized she couldn't give enough time to exercise without sacrificing some other hobbies.

benefit (noun/verb), **beneficial** (adj)
A boon or advantage that helps an individual. An element with a positive quality that offers positive gain or advantage.
A well-balanced breakfast is always beneficial, and exercise will improve your overall mood.

to empower (verb)
To give power to be able to take a particular action.
We should continue to empower children to make their own choices.

environment (noun) / **environmental** (adj)
Area or surrounding in which living organisms dwell. Correlating to the natural world.
We need to improve our safety protocols in order to protect the wildlife's environment from human expansion.

to prescribe (verb)
To advise or to authorize the use of medication by a health professional or to ask for an action or rule to be carried out.
The doctor prescribed a strong medication to improve my Grandma's heart problem.

to swell (verb), **swollen** (adj)
To increase in size due to an accumulation of liquid, or to grow by a considerable amount.
In the last few months, the refugee population has swelled unchecked and with no end in sight.

hygiene (noun), **hygienic** (adj)
Keeping clean and healthy. Maintaining health and cleanliness to prevent damaging results.
During the pandemic, we had to focus on hand hygiene first, wear masks, and keep windows open to stay safe.

clean (adj), **cleanliness** (noun)
To exhibit an absence of dirt and grime. Keeping oneself neat and tidy.
I'm doing my best to follow a clean diet, free of processed foods.

cohesion (noun), **cohesive** (adj)	To be kept together and joined in a union; integration. *Communities should encourage more outdoor activities to promote cohesion amongst neighbours.*
to adapt (verb), **adaptive** (adj)	To be able to comply with the conditions of any set element or situation. To alter in order to be suitable, repurpose. *Migrants must always find ways to adapt to new environments and cultures.*
hearty (adj)	Describes someone who is boisterous, cheerful, enthusiastic, and loud; or something which offers a substantial source of nourishment. *Dad sure knows how to make a hearty meal to fill our stomachs after a hard day's work.*
hale and hearty (id)	Describes strength and being healthy. *Even in his twilight years, he appears hale and hearty, and full of life.*
in fine fettle (id)	In very good health or condition. *The last time I saw her she was in fine fettle, despite her recent illness.*
to respond to treatment (phrase)	Expected positive reaction to a given medication or treatment. *Slowly but surely, the patient is responding to the treatment and progressively getting better.*
to nurse somebody (phrase)	To help or care for an individual or animal in order to help them back to health. *She nursed some puppies back to health in her vet clinic.*
to be allergic to (phrase)	Allergies to something which might include food or particular materials. An expression also used to denote you dislike something or someone. *I hate having lunch on the beach because the menu usually includes seafood, which I'm allergic to.*
to be on antibiotics (phrase)	To be on a regimen of medicine that fights micro-organisms. *Despite the terrible infection, she started getting better while on antibiotics.*
to treat an illness (phrase)	Take the necessary steps to cure a disease or illness. *After the necessary procedures, they decided to treat the illness with very invasive medication.*
to take effect (phrase)	To begin to show improvement after a treatment has been applied, or where the results of a particular action or ruling are seen. *The medication started to take effect after a week of use, just as the doctor intended.*

Identities

1 **Read through the list of words and phrases in the glossary (above). Find suitable words and phrases which could fit into one of the following categories:**

Description of conditions of the body	Reasons for going to the doctor
	ache
What patients do	What doctors do

2 **Match the two halves of each sentence to create a full proverb or slogan. When you write the full sentence, add punctuation marks where needed.**

i) When the heart is ... (Chinese proverb)   ... man learns the sweetness of health.

ii) Three diseases without shame ...(Irish proverb)   ... and you will improve your health.

iii) Limit your desires ...(Spanish proverb)   ... at ease the body is healthy.

iv) From the bitterness of disease ...(Catalan proverb)   ... love itch and thirst.

v) Our bodies are our ...   ... gardens our wills are our gardeners.

3 **Find and complete the idioms from these words. (If you need help, search online and/or ask your teacher.)**

drink, and be merry.   Never eat   No fear

                  Eat,   veggies are near.
                                                              Food

    for thought.   Feed

                                              more than you can lift.

              the need.

4 **Here are some quotations about health and wellbeing. Think carefully about them and discuss.**

i)
> The concept of total wellness recognizes that our every thoughts, words, and behaviour affect our greater health and well-being. And we, in turn, are affected not only emotionally but also physically and spiritually.
>
> *Greg Anderson (American author)*

ii)
> The secret of health for both mind and body is not to mourn for the past, not to worry about the future, or not to anticipate troubles, but to live in the present moment wisely and earnestly.
>
> *The Buddha*

iii)
> So many people spend their health gaining wealth, and then have to spend their wealth to regain their health.
>
> *A J Reb Materi (Canadian clergyman)*

perspective (noun)

A person's interpretation or point of view regarding a particular element or situation.

I wish you would also consider my perspective, yours is not the only valid opinion.

opinion (noun)

A person's consideration or feelings regarding a particular subject.

I'm guessing he decided not to voice his opinion due to his shyness.

assumption (noun)

Believing something to be true without any concrete evidence.

She made the assumption that he was a delinquent based solely on the way he dressed, little did she know, he was an award-winning chemist!

unassuming (adj)

Someone or something that doesn't stand out in any particular way.

He was so unassuming that nobody even noticed he was there.

ethics (noun)

Values, morals, and principles that influence conduct and thought.

An individual's ethics shouldn't shift with popular trends.

moral (adj)

Relating to the accepted societal standards regarding right and wrong.

The moral implications of his actions have had a negative effect on our community's values.

principle (noun)

The core basis of a belief system.

The principles of freedom were laid bare for the world to see during the demonstrations.

religious beliefs (noun)

The principles of an organized faith held strongly by followers of that faith.

John had been raised in a family with strong religious beliefs.

doctrine (noun)

A belief system taught by religions, political parties, or various other groups.

The church's doctrine dictates that people must help those in need.

a rite of passage (noun)

A ceremony held in some religions to mark progression from one stage of life to another.

Caleb was very excited for his bar mitzvah; it was a rite of passage of great importance in his family.

agnostic (noun/adj)

A person who does not follow any religion because they firmly do not believe the possibility of any religious doctrine to be true.

Although she was an agnostic herself, she still respected the beliefs of others.

atheist (noun/adj)

A person who chooses not to follow an organized religion or faith through lack of inclination rather than a firm disbelief.

Mark is an atheist, but he always drives his parents to church and helps out at fundraisers.

fundamentalism (noun)

The strictest observance, following, and total belief in some religious doctrines.

According to a study, religious fundamentalism is declining in some communities.

conviction (noun)

Beliefs or considerations strongly held by an individual.

Her convictions helped her see the project through, without deviating from the intended path.

to be well brought up (verb)

To be raised to have good moral values and ethics.

According to my teachers, being well brought up meant that I never got into trouble in school.

hypothesis (noun)

An idea or theory that reasonably explains an event or assumption.

She proposed a hypothesis that could be the cornerstone of future scientific advancement.

bias (noun)

Preference or prejudice directed at a group or individual, unfairly most of the time.

The townsfolk showed bias against foreigners.

prejudice (noun)

A preconceived notion or idea poorly based on dubious facts or reasons.

Those acts of discrimination were a disgraceful show of prejudice and intolerance.

ideology (noun)

A set of ideas and beliefs that form the basis of a particular theory or system.

The ideology behind a monarchic rule, in this day and age, has not aged well and is consistently challenged.

interpretation (noun)

Different ways in which people can view the same thing such as the message of a religious text or belief.

Mark and Farida both read the passage and had completely different interpretations as to what it meant.

code of conduct (phrase)

A set of guidelines to be followed in a particular environment or situation.

Not following the code of conduct in the workplace is a sure way to get fired.

to hold values strongly (verb)

To firmly agree with a belief, moral, or idea.

Camaraderie and voluntary work are strongly held values in our community.

popular culture (noun)

Trends and opinions among the general public at any given time.

Some elements of popular culture have seeped into our educational system.

integration (noun)

The joining or intermingling of different groups.

Cultural integration is prevalent in societies where a high number of migrants is present.

diversity (noun)

Composed of various elements or qualities.

We must remember that talking about diversity doesn't mean alienating one group because of personal bias; as its name implies, it includes a myriad of possibilities.

cultural sensitivity (noun)

The recognition and respect of different cultures and beliefs.

As an international community, we must ensure our cultural sensitivity grows to accept more cultural differences, instead of trying to stifle cultural practices by supplanting them with our own.

awareness (noun)

To have knowledge or understanding of a particular situation or element.

I hope we can convince people to recognize the dangers of driving without a seatbelt, we must raise awareness for the safety of all.

precept (noun)

Something to consider before embarking on a particular action.

The council issued a set of precepts that should be considered before proposing any new procedures.

empathy (noun)

Understanding and feeling what others feel.

I couldn't help but feel empathy for the boy, losing his new cap while riding a roller coaster must've been upsetting for him.

integrity (noun)

Showing firm convictions to honesty and ethical values.

He abhorred corruption wherever he found it, he wouldn't let anything jeopardize his integrity.

ideals (noun)

Strongly held beliefs and principles that an individual or group aspire to.

As a father, he tries to instil in his children the highest moral ideals possible, in order to raise proper citizens.

introspective (adj)

Relating to searching inside oneself to understand or reflect on something.

After detention, she appeared to be in an introspective mindset, trying to figure out what went wrong and how she felt about it all.

credence (noun)

Supporting something as being truthful.

Her statements give credence to her position on the matter.

1   **Match each word on the left to its opposite on the right. (Note that some words match with more than one opposite.)**

i)	credence	acceptance
ii)	distrust	falsity
		integration
iii)	denial	conviction
iv)	amoral	trust
v)	veracity	principled
		moral
vi)	separation	certainty

2   **Read the following idioms. Think about them and discuss the situations in which each of these idioms may be used.**

   i)   Pie in the sky.

   ii) To have a change of heart.

   iii) Old wives' tales.

   iv) To be on one's high horse.

   v)   The nose knows.

3   **These are famous quotes about beliefs and values. Share, think and discuss these quotes with your classmates.**

> "Strength does not come from physical capacity. It comes from an indomitable will".
>
> *Mahatma Gandhi*

> "Strong convictions precede great actions."
>
> *James Freeman Clarke*

4   **What is said around the world about beliefs and values? Read, think, and discuss this article with your classmates.**

   "The Shared beliefs of a divided America. What unites us?"

   The Washington Post, 17th January 2018

Identities

D Subcultures

cultural identity (noun)
Components such as ethnicity, nationality, traditions and so on; what an individual or group is represented by.
The interpretative dance was an expression of his cultural identity, which is why he tried so hard to perform it flawlessly.

cultural assimilation (noun)
Where a minority group or culture takes on the values, beliefs, and behaviour of another group.
An immigrant stops feeling like an alien when he is culturally assimilated and has adopted, adapted, and adjusted to the new culture.

counterculture (noun)
A set of values and beliefs which are different from the rest of society. A reaction to the established culture.
In society, a counterculture doesn't necessarily need to be antagonistic to be dominant, just a by-product of a rich environment.

the dominant culture (phrase)
The ruling/more significant culture in a society.
A dominant culture can sometimes alienate or segregate other minor groups, be it intentionally or not.

expat community (noun)
A group of people who originate from the same country or place and are living in the same area in a new country or place.
I was really worried about moving to a new country, but the expat community has been very welcoming.

third-culture children (noun)
Young people who are brought up in a culture that is different to their country of origin or to their parents' culture.
With an increasing number of third-culture children in the community, it is no surprise that we are becoming a more diverse society.

distinctiveness (noun)
Uniqueness or individuality which makes something or someone different to others.
Fashion is one of the best ways to assert your distinctiveness.

to juxtapose (verb)
To compare, or to put side by side.
It is really interesting to juxtapose different cultures, in order to understand what they have in common, along with what makes them unique and different.

tribe (noun)
A group of people who have something in common or who behave in the same way.
Urban tribes' customs vary from culture to culture.

sense or **feeling of belonging** (noun)
To be totally comfortable and happy in a place or within a group.
He felt a real sense of belonging when he joined the local history club.

connection (noun)
Something a person or group has in common with another person or group.
They got on with each other so well because they had so many connections.

unique (adj)
The only one of its kind.
People are in a constant search of qualities that make them distinct, being unique is part of our inherent nature.

to label (verb)
To describe someone in a particular way, which can be seen as unfair or untrue.
Labelling somebody because of clothes, habits, or culture does not take into account that this person is somebody who is constantly changing and developing.

ignorant (adj)
Lacking knowledge, education and/or awareness.
Her ignorant comments lost her the respect of many people who support the educational reforms.

tolerance (noun)
The ability to accept ideas or positions different to your own without having to agree with them.
No amount of tolerance can withstand continuous unabashed discriminatory slurs.

rebellious (adj)
Something that is deliberately done to undermine or insult, usually a reaction to a set of rules or norms in a society.
The students were involved in a rebellious protest about the new regulations last week.

to adjust to a different set of values (verb)	To adapt to and adopt a different set of values or to learn to fit with them.
	Creating a family and adjusting to a different set of values is not an easy task for any young couple.

xenophobic (adj)	Relating to prejudice or distaste directed at people from other nationalities or countries.
	His xenophobic comments do a disservice to the community he tries to represent through his opinions.

to alienate (verb)	Forced segregation or isolation of an individual or group through superficial, offensive, or damaging reasons.
	Through insensitive practices and commentaries, they started to alienate a group of individuals who just wish to work hard.

clique (noun)	An exclusive group of individuals who share tastes and ideas and do not usually welcome newcomers to the group.
	High schools usually have various different social cliques for teenagers to find a sense of belonging.

to isolate (verb)	To separate a person, group, or place from others so that they/it remains alone.
	Communities all around the world were forced to isolate because of the pandemic; ensuring the world must do away, hopefully temporarily, with some traditional close-contact traditions.

peer pressure (noun)	When a person feels forced to do something they wouldn't choose to do because other people are doing it.
	He only went to the party because of peer pressure, otherwise he wouldn't have been there.

to marginalize (verb)	To treat individuals, groups, identities, concepts, and so on as insignificant or worthless.
	Isolated communities tend to marginalize outsiders or people who don't comply with their ways.

Vocabulary practice

1 These verbs and phrases are made up of synonyms and opposites (or antonyms). Look carefully at them:

to hide	to create	to make a secret known	to keep out of sight
	to forge	to reveal	to divulge	to conceal

i) Find a synonym and an opposite of the verb to *disclose*.

Verb	Synonym	Opposite
to disclose		

ii) Look at the remaining verbs/phrases in the list again. Now put them into three pairs of synonyms.

Verb	Synonym

2 Fill the gaps in the following passage. Use the words from the glossary (above) to help you.

Some artists love to remain secretive and _____ their true identity. In fact, for some, like English graffiti artist Banksy, you could argue that the mystery of who he is is a large part of his success. He is entirely anonymous. We don't know his real name. He's worked to _____ his very own identity, and through his artwork and political messaging, we all have our own image of who he is. We all love mystery, of course, but he might have to give up this anonymity and _____ his identity, so that he can claim copyright and ownership of his work. But will this enigmatic person truly reveal who he is – or will he simply _____ an entirely new identity.

3   Match each word on the left with a synonym on the right.

i)	ignorant	be in agreement with
ii)	dissimilitude	being different
iii)	divergence	not similar
iv)	to side with	isolate
v)	alienate	uneducated

4   Share, think, and discuss these quotes with your classmates.

> "Clothes will disguise a fool, but his voice will give him away."
>
> *Unknown proverb*

> "Tell me whom you love, and I'll tell you who you are."
>
> *Old African proverb*

> "Every culture, or subculture, is defined by a set of common values, that is, generally agreed-upon preferences. Without a core of common values, a culture cannot exist, and we classify society into cultures and subcultures precisely because it is possible to identify groups who have common values."
>
> *Kenneth E Boulding*

> "I am one of the writers who wish to create serious works of literature which dissociate themselves from those novels which are mere reflections of the vast consumer cultures of Tokyo and the subcultures of the world at large."
>
> *Kenzaburo Oe*

5   These articles will help you to expand your vocabulary when discussing and writing about subcultures. Share, discuss, and think about these articles with your classmates:

"Am I rootless, or am I free? Third culture kids' like me make it up as we go along."
Ndela Faye
The Guardian, 9th March 2016

CALIFORNIA VAPING: THE NEW SUBCULTURE.
Owen Bennett Jones
BBC News, Los Angeles, 6th April 2015

Inside the secret world of Millennial subcultures
Tim Boyd
Financial Review, 24th January 2020

E Language and identity

idioms (noun)
Figurative non-literal expressions that come from, and are distinctive to, particular cultures.
Idioms are some of the most colourful forms of expression of any given culture and are a fantastic way of getting in touch with the language and traditions of a place.

dialect (noun)
A form or variation of language specific to a particular region or group.
The Romani people tend to have very peculiar dialects formed from many different languages, which is at the core of their identity as nomadic culture.

accent (noun)
A particular form of pronunciation of a language associated with regional variations and/or social class.
Since he moved from country to country as he was growing up, he has quite an unusual accent when speaking in English.

implied meaning (noun)
A suggested statement not directly expressed.
We are left to wonder what the implied meaning behind such a disrespectful letter was.

slang (noun)
Informal expressions and words that are part of a particular group's way of expressing themselves.
It can be difficult for older generations to understand teenagers these days because of all the slang they use!

connotation (noun)
A word or sentence with an additional meaning different from its literal meaning, which usually evokes a particular feeling or idea.
The connotations behind the words used in his letter, seemed to have an intended negative effect.

abusive language (noun)
Insulting or offensive words.
He had a troubled childhood, constantly subjected to abusive language by his peers.

collocation (noun)
Words that are grouped together for a particular reason.
Collocations are groups of words which denote a similar meaning and relevance to a context.

mind your language (phrase)
Being careful and tactful when using a particular type of language or words; a way of asking someone to speak properly and politely.
Please mind your language in front of your grandparents, it's important you show them respect.

plain language (noun)
Use of language which is easy to understand and avoids confusion and particular connotations.
Plain language is commonly used in written instructions, in order to avoid any confusion or misinterpretation.

bilingual/trilingual (noun)
Ability to use two/three languages fluently.
Thankfully, my parents brought me up to be bilingual, so I feel well-equipped for working life.

multilingual (noun)
Able to use several languages fluently.
Since she is multilingual, Keisha can give tours of the city in many different languages.

first language (noun)
The language that an individual has been learning/speaking since birth.
Even though I wasn't born in the UK I consider English my first language, since it was the only language I knew growing up.

second/third language (noun)
Other languages learned by a person later on in life.
Speaking a second language can be of great value to potential employers.

nickname (noun)
An alternative name that a person or place is known by.
He was known by the nickname 'Smiler' because he was always such a happy person.

to adopt (verb)
To take, use, or follow something.
In order to successfully integrate into a new society, people must be willing to adopt some of the customs and traditions.

master (verb)
To understand something completely, to have great proficiency, to be an expert in something.
He was able to master five languages by his tenth birthday – what an incredibly proficient student!

affable (adjective)
Easy to get along with, good-natured.
I guess she was affable enough to get along with everyone at the meeting.

personality (noun)
An individual's character formed from all his inherent qualities, behaviours, ideas, etc.
She said she couldn't stand his personality; he was too childish for her taste.

character (noun)
Qualities inherent to an individual's personality.
My cousin has a set of very distinct negative qualities to her character that make her hard to get along with.

to look like someone (verb)
To have similar physical features to another person.
People thought the two friends were related because they looked so much like each other.

to take after someone (verb)
To behave, act or do something in a similar way to another person, usually a family member.
Wow! Jac did so well in the swimming gala, she must take after her Dad!

family tree (noun)
A diagram showing the generations of a family and how they are linked.
We were able to uncover that there are cousins in Australia thanks to researching the family tree.

sexual orientation (noun)
How a person chooses to identify their preferences in intimate relationships.
Discrimination on the grounds of sexual orientation is not permitted.

heritage (noun)
A reference to the historical and cultural factors that have an input on a person's character
He feels very proud of his cultural heritage and believes it is an important part of who he is today.

to uncover (verb)
To discover something secret or not previously known.
Through cunning and careful sleuth work, he uncovered the truth about the murder.

to reminisce (verb)
To recall past events fondly.
I really enjoyed our afternoon, having the opportunity to reminisce about summer camp was lovely.

memories (noun)
Recollections of past events.
Looking at the photo album brought back many happy memories.

personal history/ experiences (noun)
Things that have happened to an individual in their lifetime.
His anger is understandable when you consider his personal history.

1 Match the words on the left with words of similar meanings on the right. (Note: You can use one word more than once.)

i)   prove   history
ii) heritage   unique
iii) uncover   reveal
iv) distinctive   discover
v)   disclose   verify

2 Read through the list of words and phrases in the glossary (above). Put the words below into the correct group according to whether they relate to written or spoken language. (Note: Some words can fit into both categories.)

Spoken language	Written language

native   talk   eloquent   to be proficient in   to master
flowery   command   idioms   fluent   accent
inspirational   slang   plain   abusive

3 These are well-known quotations said by Oliver W Holmes and Ralph W Emerson. Order the words, then think about and discuss the quotes with your classmates.

i)   stone / building / human / city / a / a / is / the / which / brought / every / language / to / of / being

ii) run / is / they / the / the / which / which / and / of / of / soul / language / blood / into / thoughts / grow / out

Identities

Experiences

A Leisure activities

recreation (noun)
An activity done for enjoyment; this can be a sport, hobby or interest.
It's good to factor in time each week for recreation as well as studying.

amateur (noun/adj)
A person who does a sport or hobby for enjoyment and is not paid to participate.
As an amateur boxer, Sam went running daily to maintain his stamina.

professional (noun/adj)
A person who is gifted at a sport or skill and is paid to play the sport or use their skills as a job.
Lara never imagined she'd be good enough to become a professional swimmer.

to cope with (verb)
To deal successfully with something difficult.
Playing lots of sports and running regularly helps me cope with the stress of my studies.

motive (noun)
A reason for doing, or desire to do, something.
Her motive for playing football was to join a team and make friends.

self-realization (noun)
Reaching your potential.
He felt a big sense of self-realization after he won the player of the season trophy.

satisfying (adj)
To fulfil a pleasure, desire or need.
Exercise helps to reduce stress and can be a satisfying release from work or study.

contributor (noun)
A person who assists someone with something in a particular way.
As the player with the most goals that season, Smith was a huge contributor to the team's success.

boost (noun)
An improvement or increase.
Getting a new pet improved her well-being significantly; being able to play with him during her spare time was a huge boost to her morale.

therapeutic (adj)
Something that contributes to a person's wellbeing, generating a good effect on the body and/or mind.
After a few tai chi sessions which were good therapeutic physical exercise, she started to improve significantly.

diversion (noun)
An activity that allows people to be distracted from stressful or tedious things.
Going kayaking is one of our favourite diversions, especially when we have a heavy workload to cope with.

amusement (noun)
Something humorous, enjoyable or funny.
Listening to your cousin's stories about the rugby tournament was such an amusement.

idle (adj)
A person who is lazy or a machine that is not used for purpose.
Maria didn't understand why such expensive machines were installed at the gym and then left idle.

to ease (verb)
To reduce the degree of an unpleasant situation.
She decided to ease tension by engaging in some relaxing yoga sessions.

to unwind (verb)
To relax, usually after having done something stressful or difficult.
She loved to go for a walk along the beach to unwind after a long day.

break (noun)
Time out from doing something else for a longer period of time.
He granted himself a long break from his work in order to focus on his studies.

respite (noun)
A period of rest.
Sanjay couldn't play in the team for six weeks because the physiotherapist said he needed respite to recover from his knee injury.

breathing space (noun)
A short break from an activity or situation before coming back to it.
The thunderstorms allowed some breathing space for the rugby players to rest and consider their tactics for the next match.

time to kill (phrase)	A fixed amount of time in between events or activities with no general purpose, other than to wait for something to take place, which can therefore be used to do something unexpected.
	We have some time to kill before the tournament, want to go get some lunch?
spare time (noun)	Time that a person has available to do what they wish to do and not what they're obligated or expected to do.
	I guess I have some spare time in my schedule to go to that yoga class.
'rest and relaxation' (or R & R) (noun)	An undefined period of time dedicated to de-stressing.
	Liv couldn't wait to get to the health spa for some well-deserved R & R.
at your convenience (phrase)	To do something at a time that suits you which does not interfere with anything else you are doing.
	Sure, we can meet tomorrow at your convenience. I'm free most of the day anyway.

Vocabulary practice

1 Each word on the left can be followed by a word on the right. Match them up. (Use each word only once.)

i)	spare	needs
ii)	cope	with
iii)	therapeutic	game
iv)	response	time
v)	satisfy	moment
vi)	satisfying	session

2 Match the two parts of the sentences to find proverbs.

i) (Albanian proverb)
    A life of leisure   what we repent at leisure.

ii) (Chinese proverb)
    To be for one day entirely at leisure   but honesty can wait a fair leisure.

iii) (German proverb)
    We do in haste   and a life of laziness are two different things.

iv) (Danish proverb)
    Deceit is in haste   and repent at leisure.

v) (Dutch proverb)
    Marry in haste   is to be for one day an immortal.

3 Here are some useful articles. Read, think about, and discuss these with your classmates.

Morning run or evening walk? Here's the science on the best time of the day to exercise.

Gretchen Reynolds

The Irish Times, 1st February 2021

Ten Unusual Museums Around the World

Hindustan Times, 26th January 2021

B Holidays and travel

trip (noun)
A vacation or visit to a place or attraction.
We are going on a trip to your favourite theme park, kids!

journey (noun)
A path or route from one place to another.
Often, the value is not in the destination, but in the journey itself!

voyage (noun)
A journey, usually involving travelling by sea or into space.
Your voyage on board our most modern cruise ship will begin at the Port of Southampton.

cruise (noun)
A holiday on a large passenger ship.
My grandparents went on a cruise to celebrate their anniversary, they particularly enjoyed all the islands they visited.

package holiday (noun)
A holiday deal that includes travel, accommodation, excursions, food, entertainment, etc, organized by a travel agent.
The agency booked us a package holiday that included a visit to the local museum, it was lovely!

jet lag (noun)
Tiredness as a result of travelling, usually from one time zone to another.
We slept through most of the first day of our holiday because of the jet lag!

travel sickness (noun)
Feeling unwell as a result of travelling, sometimes known as 'motion sickness'.
Dina loved going on holidays but always hated the journey because of her travel sickness.

tour (noun)
Travelling around various places for enjoyment.
We decided to take a tour around the city and see the sights it had to offer.

to sightsee (verb)
To visit places of interest in a location.
She went to Rome, mostly to sightsee, as she was interested in the historical buildings.

excursion (noun)
A visit to a specific place for a specific reason.
We decided to go on an excursion to explore the cave system below the mountain.

hostel (noun)
A low-cost, low-budget lodging for travellers, students, etc.
That downtown hostel is a very low-cost alternative to the expensive hotels around here, but the food is rather dismal.

ecotourism (noun)
Holidays that have a focus on environmental protection or preservation.
Ecotourism in Costa Rica has brought wealth to the local economy and helped the turtle population to recover in their natural habitat.

loss of biodiversity (noun)
A reduction in the animal and/or plant species in a given area.
Clearing of land to build large hotels on the island has contributed greatly to the loss of biodiversity in the area.

environmental impact (noun)
An effect on the natural surroundings, usually negative.
One of the worst environmental impacts of tourism is the amount of litter, particularly plastics, left on beaches.

time off (noun)
A period of rest and enjoyment, away from obligations or responsibilities such as work.
I decided to take some time off and visit my daughter, she will be very excited.

sabbatical (noun)
A fixed period of leave for a worker or educator, in order to engage in study or travel.
She spent her sabbatical studying Latin and doing a bit of travelling around Italy.

in the interim (phrase)
During the time in between two actions, activities, or events.
In the interim, the tourists exchanged pleasantries and chatted before the tour carried on.

trek (noun)
A hard journey, usually done by foot.
We decided to take a trek down to the creek. It was hard, but very rewarding.

globetrotter (noun)
A person who travels extensively.
When she was younger, my grandma was a globetrotter – she even went to India twice!

wanderlust (noun)	A strong desire to see and experience other places around the world.
	A sense of wanderlust stirs inside me whenever I see photos of exotic shores.
pilgrimage (noun)	A journey taken by people specifically to visit a sacred or holy site.
	The faithful go on a pilgrimage to the holiest of sites every summer to pay their respects.
to traverse (verb)	To pass through a place as part of a journey.
	We had to cross the river and traverse the forest on foot.
to hurtle (verb)	To move at high speed, typically in an uncontrolled manner.
	The tram hurtled through the tracks before crashing into the safety barricade, luckily no one got hurt.
to trudge (verb)	To walk very slowly, usually through exhaustion or lack of energy or in difficult conditions such as snow or mud.
	He trudged along the muddy forest paths until eventually he found the cabin.

Vocabulary practice

1 Find as many words as you can from the list (above) that belong in each group.

Tourists' actions	*Ways of travelling*

2 Find a word from the list (above) to match each definition.

i) To travel by boat.

ii) A heavy way of walking.

iii) To take a break from your job.

iv) A group of people travelling for religious purposes.

v) To visit iconic or famous places.

3 Explore and enjoy this article. Share, discuss, and think about it with your classmates:

Nine outdoor adventures to have in and around Hobart

Australian Traveller, 23rd September 2020

C Life stories

chronicle (noun)

A factual record of events in a detailed timeline

The museum made sure to have a detailed chronicle of the major events of the fifth century.

confession (noun)

Admittance of guilt over a crime or other action.

After saying the dog broke the flowerpot, we got a confession out of our son where he admitted he broke it while playing with a ball inside the house.

account (noun)

A retelling or record of an experience or event.

His account of the events included a myriad of details not present in other reports.

to recollect (noun)

To recall something.

He tried to recollect the events to the best of his abilities, but I guess those memories will never come back.

to recall (verb)

To remember something vividly.

I hope to recall memories of this lovely day when I'm older.

ancestry (noun)

Generations of a person's family spanning back many centuries.

Looking back at his ancestry, it would appear he isn't related to royalty after all.

descendant (noun)

A member of the same family of someone who lived in an earlier generation.

She is a descendant of noble Chinese aristocrats, not that she cares about it though.

origins (*or* roots) (noun)

Relating to where a person comes from.

Although Charlene was French, and her parents were German, the DNA showed that she had Asian origins going back several generations.

'stages of life' (phrase)

Periods of time in a person's life which have different characteristics.

People will change and develop different opinions as they go through different stages of life.

childhood (noun)

The youngest stage of life when a person is approximately 4 years old to 12 years old.

Maya had a very happy childhood, growing up with her brother and two sisters in a small village.

adolescence (noun)

The stage of life when a person is 13 to 19 years old.

It is a proven fact that during adolescence, teenagers need more sleep.

coming of age (phrase)

When a person is officially considered to be an adult, usually in relation to their legal ability to do things such as vote.

Farida couldn't wait for spring as she would finally be able to vote for the first time since coming of age at her last birthday.

'troubled teenage years' (phrase)

Time as an adolescent when a person makes poor choices, usually in relation to crime.

It is amazing to think how far Dan has come, especially when you look back on his troubled teenage years.

'golden years' (noun)

A later stage of life where a person has retired from work and is able to relax and enjoy their time.

My grandparents decided to enjoy their golden years by travelling around the country in their caravan.

'old age' (noun)

When a person is elderly.

Without family to care for them, many people have to live in residential care in their old age.

retirement (noun)

The end of a career, job, or profession, usually due to reaching 'retirement age', but can happen earlier in life.

There was a big party to celebrate Jean's retirement after 40 years in the teaching profession.

childhood sweetheart (noun)

A person whom somebody loved as a child or adolescent.

David and Julia were childhood sweethearts who met up again in their thirties and then got married.

biography (noun)

The story of someone's life written by a dedicated author (can also be a literary genre).

Last year, we studied both biographies and autobiographies as literary genres in our literature course at school.

autobiography (noun)

The story of someone's life, written by the person themselves.

After retiring from the profession, Harry spent six months writing his autobiography which became an international bestseller.

memoir, memoirs (noun)

An account or story of the past, taken from the recollections of the author.

His memoirs on the major events of the past decade are a national treasure.

longevity (noun)

To have the ability to be long-lasting.

The fact that the book is loved by so many generations gives it a longevity we haven't seen since Shakespeare!

'a slice of life' (phrase)

A realistic take on everyday life by movies, series, books, etc.

The book intends to show a slice of life in the suburbs.

anecdote (noun)

An account of an instance that is being told for enjoyment.

My sister's anecdote about the horse and the bull was simply hilarious; hard to believe someone who dislikes animals would enjoy spending time with them so much.

urban myth (noun)

An untrue story about a person or event that is well known by people in a particular place.

When I was young, I believed in a story about a boy who lived down near the town centre, who cried every full moon because he was abandoned there a hundred years ago; now I know it was just an urban myth.

folk tale (noun)

A story originating from popular interactions, conveyed by word of mouth.

Some of our town's folk tales focus on the abandonment of loved ones, as a blatant allegory to guilt trip youths into staying in town when they graduate.

'to cut a long story short' (phrase)

Skipping unnecessary details in a story to get to the main point of it.

Well, to cut a long story short, I decided to stay at home because I didn't have any money and I didn't want my friends to be paying my expenses.

tear-jerker (noun)

A story that evokes feelings of sadness or sympathy.

That movie about the lost puppy was a real tear-jerker.

'the truth is stranger than fiction' (phrase)

A phrase to illustrate the fact that some real-life events can be even stranger than fictional stories.

After last night's debacle at the party with the two clowns, you can see that truth is definitely stranger than fiction!

to spin a yarn (id)

To tell a story which is usually untrue.

My cousin used to spin a yarn about meeting an ex-president and a spy while on holiday.

true to life (phrase)

To represent, in a very accurate manner, true events or elements.

That movie about our independence was historically accurate, even the costumes were true to life!

symbolism (noun)

Embed symbols in different mediums such as art or literature to express or represent ideas.

The symbolism behind the maid in the painting clearly alludes to purity and innocence.

profile (noun)

A brief description of someone's life, career, character, etc.

Her life stories paint her profile as a prolific explorer.

1   Review the word list above to find at least three words for each category.

Phrases to describe parts of a lifetime	Phrases to describe different kinds of stories	Texts that talk about life experiences

2   These are famous quotes about life stories. Share, think about, and discuss these quotes with your classmates.

> "There is no greater gift you can give or receive than to honour your calling. It's why you were born. And how you become most truly alive."
>
> *Oprah Winfrey*, American talk show host and author

> "If you organized your life around your passion, you can turn your passion into your story and then turn your story into something bigger – something that matters."
>
> *Blake Mycoskie*, American entrepreneur

3   Explore and enjoy this article. Share, think, and discuss it with your classmates.

ELEVEN INSPIRING NEW ZEALAND WOMEN SHARE THEIR STORIES

Cheree Morrison, *This NZ Life*

rite (noun)
Specific parts of a ceremony usually carried out in a particular order.
They performed some of the main funeral rites for the departed yesterday.

ritual (noun)
An event of importance to those who practise it, be it religious or ceremonial, that adheres to predetermined norms and motions.
Reciting vows during a wedding ceremony is a timeless ritual that signifies both a promise and a strong verbal commitment between two people.

passage (noun)
Transitioning from one state to another or from one place to another.
The main determiner of the passage from childhood to adulthood is experience.

initiation (noun)
Some sort of entry ritual to be performed before admittance into a society or club.
For the club's initiation, we had to drink two gallons of lemonade in less than two minutes!

traditions (noun)
Beliefs and practices passed down through generations of a particular society or group.
A lovely, age-old tradition, that has been passed down through countless generations, is to show affection with a red rose.

bullying (noun)
Actions intended to intimidate or subdue a peer through detrimental physical or psychological actions.
Victims of bullying are prone to develop some deep psychological issues when they become adults.

to confer upon (verb)
The granting of a title, usually signifying a great achievement.
They decided to confer upon him the title of 'captain', in recognition of all his hard work for the team.

to commemorate (verb)
To mark or celebrate a special event.
To commemorate the tenth anniversary of the business last Friday, they gave the first ten customers a free bouquet of roses.

formality (noun)
A conventional form of an established action or process.
The ceremony was just a formality, he was already a man when he started to provide for his family since his father passed away.

to act (verb)
To do something in a particular way or for a specific purpose.
After getting the vaccine, he decided to act in a very irresponsible manner despite the health warnings.

practice (noun)
Something regularly done as a habit, custom or tradition.
Some of the most common practices around the world are rooted in deep-seated traditions.

reverence (noun)
Profound respect towards someone or something.
Despite believing in a different religion, she showed great reverence to our customs and traditions during one of our most sacred rituals.

gruelling (adj)
Very exhausting, difficult, and/or challenging.
After their gruelling rite of passage, these boys are ready to become men of our tribe!

legacy (noun)
Something that is inherited from a predecessor.
The legacy of our ancestors lives on inside us, motivating us to overcome the same rites of passage they had to face.

2 Experiences

1 **Choose which word makes sense in each of the following:**

   i)   to bully
       account   **somebody**

   ii) to commemorate
       to trek   **somebody**

   iii) to cope with
       to act   **something**

   iv) memory
       to recall   **something**

2 **Match the words on the left to the words on the right that have similar meanings.**

   i)   new beginning   celebrate
   ii) reverence   fresh start
   iii) retire   first appearance
   iv) debut   respect/admiration
   v)   commemorate   stop working

3 **Explore and enjoy. Read, think, and discuss this article with your classmates.**

   Rites of passage. Special occasions are still special.

   Melissa Kirsh

   The New York Times, 27th January 2021 (updated 29th January 2021)

E Customs and traditions

convention (noun)
An accepted traditional manner of doing something.
Brushing your teeth before going to sleep is a healthy convention that we should all follow.

folklore (noun)
Traditions, customs, stories, and anecdotes passed down orally through generations.
These beautiful songs are part of the folklore of our town, each telling the story of its foundation and humble beginnings.

belief system (noun)
A group of principles that form the basis of religion, philosophy, ideology, etc.
People tend to form complex belief systems around ideas that might not have been intended to be interpreted in such a way.

established (adj)
Something accepted and respected because of its long-standing traditional existence.
There are some established practices that are so limiting, some people prefer to do away with some of their beliefs entirely.

protocol (noun)
A formal system of rules to be followed on certain occasions.
Weddings include a series of very specific protocols that tend to be inherent to different belief systems.

'in a particular fashion' (phrase)
A specific way of doing things.
Traditional ceremonies are usually carried out in a particular fashion.

pattern (noun)
A fixed order in which something happens, is done or is organized. When the order is repeated, a pattern is formed.
The way in which things happen in most traditional customs usually follows a pattern that has been established over many years.

second nature (noun)
Something that can be done easily without having to think much about it because it's very familiar to the person.
Knowing how to use electronic devices has become second nature to most teenagers of this generation.

quirk (noun)
A particular habit or element of someone's personality or character.
The fact that she held traditional values so strongly was one of the quirks he loved most about her.

peculiar (adj)
Something that is unusual or unexpected.
It was very peculiar to see the church so empty on a Sunday.

manners (noun)
A set of conventional ways to behave in various situations.
In most ways, good manners do show how a person has been raised and what values they hold.

customary (adj)
Long-established traditional belief or way of behaving.
It is customary in Japan for people to remove their shoes when entering a home.

special occasion (noun)
A celebration of something that doesn't happen regularly such as a family gathering for a birthday or wedding.
He had a wonderful time at the party, it was a special occasion he'd never forget.

to get dressed up (verb)
To wear special clothes or a costume for a special occasion or ceremony.
It was lovely to see the guests so dressed up for the wedding celebration.

public holiday (noun)
A date upon which citizens of a country are permitted a day off work, sometimes the date commemorates an important event in history.
Everyone in the town was looking forward to the family picnic they planned for the public holiday the following week.

insular (adj)
When a person is only interested in their own country or group's ideas and rejects those of foreign entities outside those circles.
Her insular attitude stops her from being able to connect easily with others in this globalized world we live in.

tribe (noun)	A group of people that share a cultural experience in their beliefs, history, language and ways of doing things.
	Indigenous people who don't live in large cities or settlements tend to organize their societies into distinct tribes, with their unique cultures and traditions.
preservation (noun)	The protection or conservation of something so it can stay as it is and avoid decay.
	Great steps have been taken into consideration to ensure the preservation of our traditions.
to recount (verb)	To retell a story or describe something that happened in the past.
	While recounting his adventures, he stumbled upon a very old book his tribe had inherited from their ancestors.
backdrop (noun)	An established situation in which events unfold.
	Her story was told against the backdrop of civil unrest in her city.
habit (noun)	A common tendency or form of behaviour. People can have good habits or bad habits.
	The family were so accustomed to removing their shoes at home that it became a habit and the children did it everywhere they went.
ethnology (noun)	The study of different societies and cultures.
	We hired a professional who specialized in the ethnology of the region to help us better understand the local culture.

Vocabulary practice

1 **Pair up each word on the left with a word on the right. Then choose three of the pairs and write a sentence about customs or traditions using those words.**

i)	community	giving
ii)	gift	manners
iii)	sharing	happiness
iv)	bad	food
v)	good	spirit
vi)	spread	habit

2 **Reorder these words to create a proverb. Then discuss what they mean with a classmate.**

 i) the / the / to / teach / young / old / cannot / tradition (Beninese Proverb)

 ii) the / the / country / follow / flee / or / customs (Zulu Proverb)

3 **Explore and enjoy this article. Read, think about, and discuss it with your classmates.**

Seven international New Year's Eve traditions to try at home this year
Natalie B Compton
The Washington Post, 28th December 2020

colonization (noun)

When a country settles and controls a territory in another country.

Through colonization, many indigenous cultures lost their traditional way of engaging with one another.

border (noun)

A point at which two countries meet, which can be on land or at sea and is usually shown on maps as a solid line.

There was a delay when we had to wait to show our passports at the border, but otherwise the journey was hassle-free.

barriers (noun)

An obstacle or limitation set in place to control or deny access to something.

The barriers were put in place to ensure social distancing between passengers.

diaspora (noun)

The spread or dispersion of people away from their original homeland.

The displacement of people due to conflict has created several diasporas throughout history.

to transfer (verb)

To move from one place to another.

The war criminals were transferred to detainment camps to await their judgement.

exodus (noun)

A mass departure of people.

A mass exodus only shows the horrible conditions they've been facing in their home country.

migration (noun)

The movement of people from one place to another, usually to relocate in another region or country.

Rural to urban migration is increasing in many less economically developed countries.

emigration (noun)

The movement of people out of a country to live in another country.

The emigration process was riddled with complications and an absurd amount of paperwork.

immigration (noun)

The movement of people into a country from another country.

The rate of immigration into some countries is putting a strain on local resources.

deportation (noun)

Being forced to leave a country.

Some immigrants were deported back to their home countries because they didn't have the correct paperwork.

expatriate (noun)

An individual who willingly decided to live in another country away from his homeland. Often shortened to 'expat'.

Living as an expatriate in this country has given her the opportunity to learn much about different cultures around the world.

foreigner (noun)

A person who comes from another country, different from yours.

Many foreigners come during summer to enjoy our lovely beaches.

racism (noun)

Abuse of other people based on their ethnicity.

Racism in any form should not be tolerated in modern society.

outlander (noun)

A stranger or foreigner.

After three years away from my home, I still feel like an outlander.

influx (noun)

The arrival of a large group of people.

The influx of tourists has decreased significantly due to the pandemic.

depopulation (noun)

Reduction of a population in a specific area.

The leak of harmful chemicals has led to a large depopulation of the surrounding areas.

displacement (noun)

The transfer of a group of people forcefully or due to specific circumstances.

The ongoing conflict has caused the displacement of large groups of people who are now refugees.

refugees (noun)

People who have to leave their home country forcefully due to persecution, war or natural disaster.

Many refugees lost their homes in the floods and are currently living in a camp in a neighbouring country awaiting humanitarian aid.

poverty (noun)

A state of having very little or no money or possessions.

Refugees are often found living in a state of severe poverty.

settlement (noun)	A previously unoccupied area where people establish a community.
	Most of the great cities around the world started out as simple settlements that grew exponentially over time.
to resettle (verb)	To move to live in a different place.
	The leading effort for resettlement of refugees was led by the international community to ensure safety and stability in the region.
to extradite (verb)	Turn over an accused criminal to the authorities of a foreign nation where they committed a crime.
	Criminals who have been extradited usually face harsher sentences than they would face in their home countries.
to squat (verb)	To live in or occupy a building or piece of land illegally.
	After the conflicts calmed down, some people decided to start squatting in abandoned homes.
to part (verb)	To leave someone's company.
	They decided to part on good terms, even though they had some issues in the past.
to exile (noun)	Banning people from re-entering their home country mostly for political or punitive reasons.
	She retold her story of being exiled in a very strange land.
to ostracize (verb)	The exclusion of a person from a group or society.
	He was ostracized by many of his friends because of his illegal dealings during his tenure as governor.
to relegate (verb)	To be assigned to an inferior position or rank.
	After he failed the language exam, he was relegated to a lesser paid position within the company.
changeover (noun)	A total shift from one system, method, or situation, to another.
	The changeover in policy benefited plenty of migrants.

Vocabulary practice

1 All of these words relate to migration. Match the words on the left to their opposite on the right.

i)	voluntary	illegal
ii)	international	temporary
iii)	permanent	forced
iv)	documented	immigrant
v)	emigrant	national
vi)	legal	undocumented

2 Look at these groups of words. Find the odd one out in each group.

i)	barrier	asylum	border	frontier
ii)	diaspora	arrival	exodus	depopulation.
iii)	shift	move	migrate	settle

3 Each of the following words can either precede or follow the word 'refugee'. Write out the words and decide if 'refugee' should be written before or after each one.

i) _____ camp _____   iv) _____ economic _____

ii) _____ political _____   v) _____ flow _____

iii) _____ status _____

4 Explore and enjoy. Listen to this podcast. Then discuss your thoughts on it with a classmate.

'A New Normal'
From *SE 15 Productions*

Human ingenuity

A Entertainment

celebrity (noun)
A person who is very well-known and easily recognized by the public due to their fame.
As a celebrity, she enjoyed great perks and fame that others could only dream of.

starlet (noun)
A young actress who hopes to become a leading actress when she is older.
As a starlet, she played some minor roles in low-budget series.

famous (adj)
A person who is known by many, often worldwide.
She was a young starlet who dreamed of one day being a famous leading lady.

stardom (noun)
The state in which one is recognized as being a famous celebrity.
Thanks to his stardom, he was able to help those in need through charities and sponsorships.

performance (noun)
A piece of entertainment such as a play, a presentation, dancing, or singing.
During their performance, they considered using a crane and various stunt doubles to perform high-risk stunts!

stunt (noun)
A difficult feat requiring skill and daring. Actors are sometimes replaced by trained professionals called 'stunt doubles' for dangerous stunts in movies.
Even though he got injured performing his last stunt, he refused to use a stunt double and was ready to try again.

extravaganza (noun)
An elaborate piece of entertainment or production.
A performance like this was to be expected, an "over-the-top" extravaganza that included tigers and daring acrobatics.

spectacle (noun)
A notable or unusual piece of entertainment.
Seeing the show go so badly wrong was quite a spectacle!

to broadcast (verb)
To transmit through streaming, television, radio, etc.
The band's performance was broadcast to every corner of the world in a midnight stream that dazzled audiences.

pantomime (noun)
1 A stage play, usually based on a children's story, told in a comical way with lots of visual humour and often including music and dancing. Pantomimes are often performed at Christmas.
The family went to see the pantomime, Aladdin, at the Empire Theatre as a Christmas treat.

2 An event or situation that is extremely comical or ridiculous.
The removal firm made such a mess of packing the van that it became a pantomime to watch!

musical (noun/adj)
1 (noun) A stage play or film that tells a story which develops through song and dance as well as dialogue.
Lea thought she didn't like musicals, until she saw The Greatest Showman.

2 (adj) Someone or something that is tuneful.
Her musical humming could be heard in the background during the rehearsal, which annoyed the director.

drama (noun)
1 A television series, film or play that is characterized by a plot involving serious conflict, tone, or subject matter.
The high-school drama about an impoverished teen won several awards at the film festival.

2 An event or situation that is highly emotional.
It was a real drama when we thought Jack was missing. Turned out he was asleep the entire time!

melodrama (noun)
A television series, film, or play that is characterized by a plot involving everyday events which can sometimes be over exaggerated for effect.
Her play proposal could be considered a melodrama that deals with the struggles of a secretary, plagued by the horrors of answering calls and filling memos.

melodramatic (adj)
Someone or something that overreacts to a given situation or overexaggerates an emotion.
Whilst the performance was enjoyable, we thought the lead actor was very melodramatic in the wedding scene.

comedic (adj)	Someone or something that is funny.
	The famous actress guest starred in the comedic episode about spiders with party hats.
episodic (adj)	Something that happens in small parts (or episodes) such as a television or book series.
	Last year we started reading an episodic saga of pirate adventures. We can't wait for the next book to be released!
fictional (adj)	Books, shows, plays, or characters that are created by a writer and are not real.
	Some fictional characters can be more memorable than real people.
paparazzi (plural noun)	Photographers who stalk celebrities to get photos of them without their permission or prior arrangement.
	The actors didn't leave the hotel for three days because of the paparazzi waiting outside.
glamour (noun)	An appealing attractive quality that makes people or things seem exciting or interesting.
	She had always wanted to be an actress because of the glamour of Hollywood.
escapism (noun)	Doing an activity to escape reality or routine.
	She lost herself in video games as a form of escapism to run away from her obligations.
to binge-watch (verb)	To watch most or all of a television series or box set in one session.
	He decided to binge-watch two seasons of his favourite show in one night!
box set (noun)	The complete collection of all episodes or series of a television show or all instalments of a film collection.
	Her only plan that weekend was to watch the box set of her favourite crime drama.

Vocabulary practice

1 Look at these groups of words. Find the odd one out.

i)   musical   ballet   auditorium   pantomime

ii) ball   soap operas   TV serial   sensational programme

iii) social gathering   sleepover   stardom   get together

iv) distraction   dissatisfaction   recreation   amusement

v)   broadcast   talk show   cartoon   podcasts

2 Pair up the words on the left with the words on the right to make phrases to describe somebody who loves partying or is very sociable.

i)   pleasure   goer

ii)   social   animal

iii) party   butterfly

iv)   party   seeker

3 These are quotes about entertainment. Share, think and discuss these quotes with your classmates.

"I find television very educational. Every time somebody turns on the set, I go into the other room and read a book."
Groucho Marx (American comedian)

"I still get wildly enthusiastic about little things… I play with leaves. I skip down the street and run against the wind."
Leo Buscaglia (American author)

B Artistic expression

expression (noun)
The way a person conveys their emotions, opinions, or feelings.
Her artistic expression was mired in controversy after she featured some disturbing art pieces in the exhibit.

artistic (adj)
Relating to creative expression.
One could argue that his artistic genius comes from many years at work, travelling around the world and learning about different cultures.

technique (noun)
A way of doing something or the style in which an artist usually approaches their work.
His technique of blending light and shade made his paintings popular with so many people.

audience (noun)
A group of individuals gathered to watch someone speaking or performing.
The audience enjoyed the show from home because of the lockdown, with the same enthusiasm as if they were there on set!

to stage (verb)
To put on an event.
They decided to stage the performance in the atrium of the building, in order to ensure an outdoor experience and be able to properly practise social distancing.

prop (*usually plural* **props**) (noun)
An object used by performers in a play or film.
Among the props used in their performance, there was even a rubber duck!

ornate (adj)
Something that is beautifully and intricately decorated.
The stage was set with ornate gold coloured decorations that made it look like a real palace ballroom.

artistry (noun)
Great skills possessed by a person as an artist or performer.
She showcased a level of artistry in her routine that the judges had not seen in many years.

exhibition (noun)
A show for the public to attend featuring artwork, photographs or other media put together under a theme or from one artist.
Last week's highlight was an exhibition featuring modern works of art by up-and-coming artists.

installation (noun)
A piece of art, a sculpture, a photograph or other piece of work in display in a museum or gallery.
Jane spend all day arranging the new installations and was excited for the exhibition to open to the public.

iconic (adj)
A very famous or popular representation.
Some of the most iconic works of art can be seen at the Louvre in Paris.

script (noun)
The written words for a play or performance. Actors memorize their lines from the script.
Some of the most famous lines from the movie were not in the original script, in fact they were improvised by the actor.

repertoire (noun)
The music, songs, plays, roles, etc that a performer usually specializes in.
He included special songs for the anniversary concert which weren't in his usual repertoire.

muse (noun)
A source of profound inspiration.
My dad always said that while painting, my mother was his muse.

to embody (verb)
To represent a quality, idea, or belief.
Her paintings were modern in style but still embodied the beliefs of her ancestors.

idealistic (adj)
Someone who believes in positive outcomes, despite other people's doubts.
Despite numerous setbacks, he remained an idealistic activist against climate change.

recognition (noun)
Admiration and respect in acknowledgement of your achievements.
After their first exhibition, showing their radical new art style, they gained a lot of recognition and praise.

memorable (adj)
Something to be remembered or worth remembering.
Last night's performance was a memorable addition to their impeccable track record when it comes to live shows!

influential (adj)	Something that has a great effect over someone or something.
	As an influential content creator, he devoted his free time to campaigning against racism through his work.
rehearsal (noun)	A practice or run through of a performance in a private setting in order to make improvements or changes.
	The disaster of their last rehearsal didn't deter them, and they gave a memorable performance.
endorsement (noun)	Support for something or someone.
	With the foundation's endorsement, they were able to collect enough money to put on the free concert they had been planning.
rating (noun)	A measure of the quality or success of something.
	Even though the ratings confirmed their worst fears, subsequent shows ensured the popularity of the play against all odds.
review (noun)	A written report giving the opinion of the writer about something such as a play, show, or film.
	The reviews of the new play were so good that all performances sold out the next day!
recommendation (noun)	A piece of advice or a suggestion to do something.
	His latest film is top of the list of recommendations for what to watch this week.
troupe (noun)	A group of performers.
	Hearts fluttered as the dance troupe came on stage for one last time.

Vocabulary practice

1 **Look at these groups of words. Find the odd one out in each group.**
   i)   ornate, extravaganza, musical, spectacle
   ii)   cast, troupe, band, starlet
   iii) idealistic, celebrity, famous, stardom
   iv)   repertoire, prompt, rehearse, glamour
   v)   installation, ornate, recommendation, prop

2 **Complete the phrases (below) with these words. You can use the same word more than once. (If you need help, search online, and/or ask your teacher.)**

   art   blank   justice   picture

   i)   A _____ paints a thousand words.
   ii)   Fine _____
   iii) A _____ canvas
   iv)   Poetic _____
   v)   State of the _____
   vi)   In the _____
   vii) _____ for art's sake.
   viii) Get the _____
   xi)   The _____ of war.
   x)   The big _____

3 **Explore and enjoy. Share, think about, and discuss these articles with your classmates.**

   SCOTTISH MUSIC INDUSTRY WARNS IT HAS BEEN LEFT 'ON THE BRINK OF COLLAPSE'
   Brian Ferguson
   The Scotsman, 26th April 2021

   Oscar ratings drop to an all-time low with unwatchable show
   Lauren Sarner
   The New York Post, 26th April 2021

C Communication and media

announcement (noun)
New information about something.
The last announcement made by the government ensured that vaccinations will go forward, despite the setbacks caused by the pandemic in recent months.

press (noun)
Businesses that print news in newspapers or magazines and the people who work for them.
The local press was lauded for their adherence to the truth and freedom of speech.

freedom of the press (phrase)
The right of newspapers and magazines to be able to print freely without censorship.
Freedom of the press is as important as free speech.

journalism, journalist (noun)
The process of researching and writing information to be used in a newspaper or magazine article; a person who researches and writes articles for newspapers or magazines.
I am fascinated by politics and always wanted a career in journalism.

ethical journalism (noun)
Researching information in such a way that moral standards are upheld, and people's rights are not violated.
Some journalists could be underhanded and would do anything for a scoop, but the Goldman News Group was proud of their policy of ethical journalism, even if it did mean missing the occasional headline.

publication (noun)
Stories or articles in magazines, newspapers or documents.
Many of last week's publications focused on the political scandal that is dominating the headlines.

newspaper (noun)
A daily publication of news reports, articles, columns, etc. Traditionally presented on printed paper but also available online.
Our local newspaper tries its best to be an objective and reliable source of information.

article (noun)
A written piece focusing on a particular topic. Usually published in a magazine, newspaper, or the internet.
There was an article on gardening that, my mother swears, saved her orchard.

column (noun)
A newspaper or magazine article focusing on a particular topic, written in a recurrent fashion by a specific author.
Her popular sports column was a staple in our favourite newspaper.

tabloid (noun)
A type of newspaper with short reports and plenty of pictures, often full of stories about celebrities or sports with perhaps less focus on major political events.
Local tabloids depicted some pictures of a supposed love affair involving a local starlet, to the shock and dismay of many.

broadsheet (noun)
A type of newspaper with longer, more in-depth reports than a tabloid newspaper. These are also physically bigger in size.
He thought he was better than everyone else just because he read one of the broadsheets on his way to work.

headline (noun)
The title of the story or main idea presented in a newspaper, usually printed in a larger, bolder style than the text around it.
The catchy headline instantly got readers hooked, despite the lack of meaningful content.

byline (noun)
A line stating the name of the author of an article or story in a newspaper or magazine.
Sadly, they misspelt the author's name in the byline of his most famous article.

strapline (noun)
An easy-to-remember phrase associated with a brand, that makes it recognizable.
The cola company uses a very catchy strapline that is known by young people and adults alike.

advertisement (noun)
Something designed to promote a product or service and influence consumers to purchase something or do something.
Sales rocketed thanks to the advertisements they placed in the major daily newspapers.

billboard (noun)
A very large advertisement, usually seen in highly populated areas, along major roads, or in busy places such as stadiums or airports.
A popular billboard depicting a bear riding a boat can be seen on our busiest highway as you head out of town.

pop-up (noun)

1 A window that appears unexpectedly during online browsing, often containing an advertisement.

A terrible virus on my laptop has caused a flood of pop-ups that plague my online browsing.

2 A new business which appears in a location on a temporary basis.

There's a new pop-up restaurant by the station, I heard an advertisement for it on the radio.

propaganda (noun)

Messages spread by the press, intended to influence the opinions of a group of people.

Political propaganda has greatly impacted the spread of reliable news.

social media (noun)

Web-based platforms where people can keep in touch, share opinions, and interact with others.

It's hard to escape fake news when social media is full of it.

vlogger (noun)

A content creator who records, in video form, his thoughts, opinions and information gathered to be shared on the internet or via social media. (Derived from the phrase video blogger.)

Last week, the popular vlogger released a video on pet care that was an instant hit with animal lovers.

influencer (noun), **influential** (adj)

Someone or something that has the ability to sway the behaviour and opinions of others.

As a fashion icon and influencer, he always shares his preferences on products with his fans on social media.

The newspaper admits that its influential columns may have affected public opinion on the matter, for which they apologized in a press release.

blog (noun)

A person's thoughts and opinions or information shared as an informal article on the internet for others to read.

He was dealing with a lot of anxiety during the quarantine, so he wrote a series of blog entries about his experience during the COVID-19 pandemic.

radio (noun)

1 Electrical equipment that can receive signals and broadcast information or music. Companies that broadcast on various signals are called radio stations.

Dad prefers to listen to the news on the radio in the car rather than watch it on TV.

2 A communication device used to make verbal contact with other people, especially when other forms of technology or communication are not available.

During the conflict, radios became a lifeline for the refugees.

mass media (noun)

A term for the collective ways of sharing information to a large number of people at any one time.

News of the approaching hurricane spread quickly thanks to coverage by mass media.

transmission (noun)

Something that is broadcast or sent out through radio, television, the internet, etc.

Various transmissions came from overseas, claiming a new threat was on the horizon.

to vocalize (verb)

To give your ideas, opinions, or feelings in the form of spoken words.

The vlogger vocalized her concerns about the new policies that may endanger some immigrants if implemented.

discourse (noun)

Discussion in spoken or written form.

Their political discourse was received with both scepticism and hope for a better outcome.

to disclose (verb)

To publicly show something that was hidden or simply something to be known.

A non-profit organization decided to disclose some damaging information on the illegal practices of some politicians, which caused quite a scandal!

to voice (verb)

To express your opinion.

Despite various warnings from her superiors, she decided to voice her concerns about the discrimination in her workplace.

networking (noun)

The process of meeting new people who might be useful to know.

After the symposium, I met some big names in the industry. I hope it was a good bit of networking on my part.

webinar (noun)

An online meeting to discuss and/or learn about a subject at a specified time.

Even though I was on a trip, I luckily found some working wi-fi to join last week's webinar on clean energy proposals.

symposium (noun)

A meeting to discuss and/or learn with people who possess great knowledge about a subject at a specified time and place.

After I left the symposium, I had more questions than answers! Can't wait for the next gathering to learn more from that master salesman.

1 **Look at the following groups of related words. Choose a word from the right-hand column to fit in each group. Working with a partner, decide what title or description you could give to each group.**

	Title or description		
i)		headline strapline byline	
ii)		withholding suppression denial	**vocalize**
iii)		broadsheet tabloid mass media	**press**
iv)		sitcoms debates series	**melodrama**
v)		virtual community language connections	**advertising** **bias**
vi)		networking meeting symposium	**article**
vii)		blog vlogger meme	**social media**
viii)		billboard promotion pop ups	**music** **webinar**
ix)		stations commercials weather forecasts	**influencer**
x)		butt in voice speak up	

2 **Match the verbs on the left to the words on the right to find phrases.**

i)   to get   the web

ii) to voice   in the spotlight

iii) to get   your wires crossed

iv) to surf   your opinion

v)   to be   straight to the point

3 **These quotes about the media are from famous works of literature. Share, think and discuss these quotes with your classmates.**

"What the mass media offers is not popular art, but entertainment, which is intended to be consumed like food, forgotten, and replaced by a new dish."

W H Auden, *The Dyer's Hand*

"Once upon a time there were mass media, and they were wicked, of course, and there was a guilty party. Then there were the virtuous voices that accused the criminals. And Art (ah, what luck!) offered alternatives, for those who were not prisoners to the mass media.

Well, it's all over. We have to start again from the beginning, asking one another what's going on."

Umberto Eco, *Travels in Hyperreality*

D Technology

gadget (noun)
A mechanical or electronic object that has a practical use and is usually time or labour-saving.
A simple gadget ensures that people can stay connected over incredibly long distances with the push of a button. A true marvel!

device (noun)
A mechanism or piece of equipment designed for a specific use or special function.
After assembling his monstrous machine, no one expected that a small, simple device was the component that ultimately kept it working.

hardware (noun)
The physical and electronic component parts of a computer.
Picking out a good piece of hardware to build a great PC is easier said than done, that's why most people settle for laptops and the like.

software (noun)
Computer programs that dictate what a computer does.
Software has evolved over the years to ensure that things like accounting, teaching and exploring, are made as simple as the push of a button.

digital (adj)
Something that is presented electronically.
Digital books are still a contentious topic of discussion, some people just can't let go of that lovely smell of a new book, or a musty old one.

system (noun)
A set of interconnected elements that work together.
Computers are integrated systems that formulate tasks on command, kind of like how our brains command our bodies.

network (noun)
A set of interconnected elements that work together to allow data or communication flow.
A new addition to the network's software ensures that people can be connected at faster speeds, with reduced delay.

wireless (adj)
Something that doesn't need to be physically connected to other devices.
Wireless software such as Bluetooth facilitates data exchange without cumbersome cables.

broadband (noun)
A type of internet connection; it ensures that large amounts of information can be shared quickly between computers.
Through wireless broadband connections, we keep data flow in constant exchange.

browser (noun)
Computer software that enables the user to surf the internet.
Websites loaded much faster after they installed a new browser.

search engine (noun)
Computer software that can quickly find specific information on the internet.
You can find out information about any travel destination by simply putting the name of the location into a search engine, like Google.

streaming (noun)
Engaging with entertainment media (sound, video, etc) directly from the internet.
Because of the pandemic, various big events and concerts can now be enjoyed through streaming in real-time!

connectivity (noun)
The ability of devices or systems to connect with one another.
You need to upgrade your software to ensure connectivity.

firewall (noun)
A piece of software designed to stop people from seeing your information on the internet.
Our company's firewall is very advanced and effective when protecting our information, but it's also very expensive!

antivirus (adj)
Software designed to delete harmful computer programs and keep your system safe and clean.
My free antivirus software actually installed some viruses into my system!

virus (noun)
A self-replicating computer program, or part of one, designed to prevent a computer from working properly.
A computer virus that doesn't allow your antivirus software to work is always a terrible nuisance.

to hack (verb)
To remotely invade another person's computer with the intention of stealing information or to plant a virus.
The company didn't even have firewalls on the computers which made them very easy to hack.

hacker (noun)

A person who has the skills to remotely invade another person's computer with the intention of stealing information or to plant a virus.

The company believed their network was protected by the best software, but it was no match for the hacker who was able to steal all their clients' data in a few simple clicks.

whiz (noun)

An informal word to describe a person with a high skill level or knowledge which enables them to do a particular task very quickly.

My best friend is a real whiz with computers and always helps me out when my laptop goes wrong!

data breach (noun)

When personal information is stolen, lost, or accidentally revealed to others without the owner's permission.

People lost faith in the company after the huge data breach last year.

phishing (noun)

An attempt to trick someone over the internet to give out their information so their money can be stolen.

Someone posing as his internet provider sent my grandpa a fake email. They were actually phishing, and he got his bank account cleaned out because they tricked him into giving his bank details.

malware (noun)

Software designed to prevent a computer from working properly.

Some pesky malware isn't letting me run my favourite game!

to encrypt (verb)

To change data or signals into a secret code for protection.

We had to encrypt our protocols because we were constantly being hacked, and our productivity was at an all-time low.

cryptography (noun)

The process of creating a code designed to keep information secret.

Our processes have been updated through a complex algorithm, supported by cryptography and innovation.

database (noun)

A digital store of information in a computer program.

The bank's database was recently hacked by criminals who had hoped to steal customer details, luckily the encrypted protocols did their job and helped us avoid catastrophe.

hi-tech (adj)

The most advanced elements and methods.

A plethora of hi-tech devices have flooded the market in the last decade, making daily tasks more efficient!

mechanization (noun)

The process of machines replacing manual labour.

Some workers have been laid off from their factory jobs due to the mechanization of some of their tasks.

to compute (verb)

To calculate or work out an answer or amount through the use of a machine.

The time it takes to compute the sales figures has halved since we went digital.

to upgrade (verb)

To improve the quality, processes, or methods of something for the better.

We decided to upgrade our medical equipment to better handle the demands of the ongoing pandemic.

to optimize (verb)

To make something work as effectively as it can.

We optimized our methods to ensure peak efficiency in our response times to emergencies.

to automate (verb)

To make something work automatically by using machines or computers.

We decided to automate our call centres so we could cut back on hiring personnel for the task, the results have been mixed so far.

1 **Complete the idioms below with one of the following words:**

wire   wire   Sputnik   button   buttons

If you need to, you can search them on the internet and/or ask your teacher if you are not sure.

i)   _____ moment

ii)   Close to the _____

iii) Press the right _____

iv)   Hold the _____

v)   Push the panic _____

2 **Choose the best adjective (on the left) to describe each noun (on the right). (Use each adjective only once.)**

i)   scientific   gadget

ii)   digital   advancement

iii) wireless   resources

iv)   electronic   kid

v)   whiz   era

3 **These articles are about technology. Share, think about, and discuss these articles with your classmates.**

WAZIRX TO COMPENSATE USERS WHO LOST BIG ON VOLATILE MEME COIN

Apoorva Mittal

*The Economic Times (*Tech News) 16th May 2021

LOCKDOWN AND TECH OVERLOAD – HOW TO ESCAPE YOUR SCREEN

Sina Joneidy and Charmele Ayadurai

The Conversation, 27th May 2020

E Scientific innovation

scientific (adj)
Relating to the fields of biology, chemistry, or physics.
The scientific community has gone through great strides to ensure that the pandemic is contained, and people can go back to some semblance of normality.

innovation (noun)
A new idea or method.
Innovation has become a hallmark of the 21st century.

advance, advancement (noun)
A development or improvement in something; a move forward.
Modern-day practices in medicine are a notable advance in comparison to older, more traditional methods.
Vaccines have been one of the most impressive scientific advancements of the last millennium.

improvement (noun)
Something that gets better or is made better.
Scientific improvements have shown that hardship can't stand in the way of knowledge and innovation.

breakthrough (noun)
An instance that provides an advancement or improvement of a problem.
New breakthroughs in molecular science have given us exciting new ways to preserve endangered species of animals.

empirical (adj)
Something based on what is actually seen instead of the theory.
Our process of experimentation has ensured that people get only the best and safest products, based on empirical evidence and quality control measures.

design (noun)
A pattern, plan, or drawing of something that is to be created.
The design of the new showroom intends to create a warm and welcoming space which will attract more customers.

invention (noun)
Something new, be it an object or method.
His latest invention was a flop that only managed to burn down his garage!

simulation (noun)
A replica of a real-life situation used for training purposes.
Virtual simulations ensure our workers can deal with any circumstance or hazard that can come their way.

to experiment (verb)
To carry out tests to discover something or prove something to be true.
Creating the COVID-19 vaccine was an intricate process, involving experiments, trials and research to ensure safety and effectiveness.

to patent (verb)
To have the legal right to produce and/or sell an invention exclusively.
John's invention worked so well that he patented it to make sure nobody else was able to steal his idea.

to brainstorm (verb)
To think quickly of new ideas or to make suggestions for a particular problem or issue.
Through various brainstorming sessions, we were finally able to agree on the name, logo and menu for the new restaurant.

vaccine (noun)
A substance containing a harmless amount of a particular virus or bacteria in order to prevent the body from actually suffering from the diseases it carries.
Even though no COVID-19 vaccine is a hundred percent effective, they seem to be successful enough to give the population some peace of mind.

isolation (noun)
When a person separates themselves physically from coming into contact with other people.
Since she was coughing so much, they asked her to spend ten days in self-isolation as a precaution.

quarantine (noun)
A period of time in which someone with a disease, or suspicion of having one, must isolate himself to prevent further spread of the disease.
Since the quarantine period started, I've decided to catch up on my reading to pass the time.

insulation (noun)

Covering something to prevent heat, sound, electricity, etc from entering or escaping.

Samples require complex methods of insulation to ensure their consistency.

drone (noun)

An unmanned aircraft that is remote controlled.

A police drone was hovering over the town centre, doing a routine sweep.

to propel (verb)

To generate movement.

Hardship propels the need for innovation.

to scan (verb)

To look at something carefully by eye or with a machine to gather information.

The drone was scanning the surrounding area to find the criminal.

to fabricate (verb)

1 To create a product.

Various medical equipment has been fabricated to meet the growing demands of hospitals.

2 To tell someone something that you know to be false.

We believed his story; little did we know he was fabricating it all.

to convert (verb)

To change from one type to another.

Many processes have been changed or converted to deal with the challenges arising due to the pandemic.

to recondition (verb)

To repair a machine or piece of equipment and bring it to a good or better condition.

You can buy reconditioned laptops and computers quite cheaply and they often work as well as buying new.

1 **Use the words below to complete these phrases related to scientific innovation. (You can search on the internet and/or ask your teacher if you are not sure.)**

   i)   biomedical _____

   ii)   big_____

   iii)   _____ additional experiments

   iv)   absolute _____

   v)   growth _____

   vi)   forward _____

   vii)   _____ improvements

   viii) ground-breaking _____

   xi)   innovative _____

   x)   major _____

breakthrough	bang
design	study
thinking	conduct
innovation	zero
mindset	continuous

2 **Choose some of the words from the list of vocabulary (above) to fit into each group in this table. What other words related to science do you know that you could add to each group?**

COVID-19 words	Verbs	Nouns	Adjectives

3 **Explore and enjoy. Read these articles then discuss them with your classmates.**

SCIENTIFIC INNOVATION IN 2021: LESSONS FROM COVID-19

Mark Kessel

Down to Earth, 9th February 2021

Five coronavirus questions scientists still don't have answers to

Dan Fox

Nature, 21st July 2020

A Social relationships

bachelor (noun)

An unmarried man.

As a bachelor, he felt quite lucky to be moving by himself to a new city full of romantic opportunities.

spinster (noun)

A woman who has never been married; now more commonly used for describing an older woman who has never been married. For a younger woman, we would normally say 'an unmarried woman'.

My aunt is a spinster and says she's never regretted not being married.

engaged (to be married) (adj)

When two people have agreed to marry each other.

When my cousin got engaged, her parents threw a party so the whole family could celebrate, and it was quite an emotional occasion.

married (adj)

A couple that has had a wedding to bind their relationship together legally and/or in line with their religion.

My grandparents are a very happily married couple; they still celebrate every anniversary as if it were their first.

divorced (adj)

To be legally separated from your married partner.

After his affair was discovered, he ended up a divorced man.

widow (f), widower (m) (noun)

Someone whose husband or wife has died, and she/he has not remarried.

Statistically, widowers in the US are up to ten times more likely than widows to remarry or enter a romantic relationship.

monogamy (noun)

A relationship with one partner only.

Practising monogamy has become a staple of western traditions.

bigamy (noun)

Being in several marriages at the same time. Bigamy is usually seen as a crime when you knowingly enter a second marriage when already married to someone else, but this is not true for some cultures.

Jane watched an interesting documentary about communities where bigamy is commonplace.

to hook up (verb)

To meet with someone in a work, social, or sexual manner.

He hooked up with a girl who turned out to be one of his classmates! They had a very awkward meeting before lectures the next morning.

affair (noun)

A secret romantic or sexual relationship usually used to describe a relationship taking place in secret whilst one or both persons is in a relationship with another person.

The politician fell out of public favour when his affair was discovered.

to be estranged (from) (verb)

To no longer hold a close relationship with someone.

She was estranged from her mother for most of her life.

affinity (noun)

A liking for someone or something based on shared characteristics.

I have a strong affinity for my grandmother because we are so similar.

correlation (noun)

A connection or relationship between two or more things.

There appears to be no correlation between his hook-ups, and his tendency to be unable to form meaningful relationships.

liaison (noun)

1 When a person acts as liaison, it is their role or job to maintain mutual communication and cooperation between groups of people.

Throughout the ongoing negotiations, the person acting as liaison did a fantastic job bringing both sides to the negotiating table.

2 A relationship or meetings with another person, usually used to describe a relationship that is in some way secretive or personal in nature.

There was a lot of gossip after his colleagues found out about his liaison with their line manager.

rapport (noun)

A relationship between people or groups.

The teacher decided that the best way to reach his students was to build a strong rapport with them.

exchange (noun)

An arrangement in which students go from one country to live with students in another.

After she came back from her exchange to Australia, she said she'd had enough sunshine to last her a lifetime!

to exchange (verb)

To share or swap thoughts, ideas, or physical items.

The class debate was a great way for students to exchange their points of view.

accord (noun)

A formal agreement.

After the accord was signed, both countries agreed to a ceasefire on humanitarian grounds.

alliance (noun)

An agreement to cooperate towards reaching the same goal.

A formal alliance was achieved after signing the peace accord between the two paramilitary groups.

to disassociate (verb)

To no longer support or have any kind of relationship with something or someone.

The vlogger decided to disassociate from that specific brand because of their unethical practices in their contracts.

division (noun)

Situation in which people show disagreement.

There appears to be a rising division between both sides of the political spectrum, at this rate, no agreement will be reached!

opposition (noun)

Strong disagreement towards a person or group, sometimes speaking or fighting against it.

The opposition fought very hard to make their voices heard and heal the growing division within the people.

interpersonal (adj)

Relating to relationships between people.

Their interpersonal relationships had no bearing on the decision made by the council.

entanglement (noun)

A situation or relationship that is difficult to get out of.

His latest legislative entanglement forced him to relinquish his seat in the senate.

kinship (noun)

A relationship with others that feels like being part of a family; having a very strong bond.

The group of friends had built up a strong kinship during their time at high school.

next of kin (noun)

The person (or persons) who is the nearest or closest relative (or relatives) to someone.

When you are admitted to hospital, it's commonplace to be asked who your next of kin are.

lineage (noun)

All the living people directly connected to common ancestors.

He could trace his lineage as far back as the Middle Ages!

fraternal (adj)

Relating to brothers or to be connected as brothers.

Their fraternal bond would not be broken by their reprehensible choices during the rugby match.

fraternal twins (noun)

Twins are two people who were born at the same time, on the same day to the same mother. If they are fraternal twins, they are not necessarily identical and may not be of the same gender. (Compare with **identical twins**.)

Despite being fraternal twins, my brother and sister have very little else in common. They regularly fight over everything at home!

identical twins (noun)

Twins are two people who were born at the same time, on the same day to the same mother. If they are identical twins, they share the same genetic characteristics (hair, eye colour, etc) and will always be the same gender.

I love being an identical twin! My sister and I look very alike so we share all our clothes which saves us a lot of money.

only child (noun)

Someone who has no brothers or sisters.

As an only child, I grew up without any other young children to keep me company, so became accustomed to finding ways to entertain myself.

orphan (noun)/**to be orphaned** (verb)

A child whose parents have both died.

The twins became orphans at the young age of 12, after their parents both died in the plane crash.

single-parent family (*or* **one-parent family**) (noun)

A family where there is only one parent (either a mother or a father) and at least one child. One parent can be described as a single parent either through death or through divorce (or separation).

In the UK, there were 2.9 million single-parent families in 2019; that number represents about 15% of all families in the country.

stepfamily (noun)

A family where the parents live as a couple and the child (or children) come from a different marriage (or relationship) so the children do not share the same parents.

I don't get on at all with my stepfather, so find it very difficult living as part of a stepfamily.

blended family (noun)

A family made up of two parents together with their stepchildren and children from the new marriage (or relationship).

A 'non-traditional' blended family is actually becoming the 'new traditional' family as more parents remarry and bring together their children under the same roof.

Vocabulary practice

1 The following suffixes can be added to 'woman' or 'man'. Add the correct suffix and find the word that fits each of the following definitions.

-ish   -like   -hood   -ly

i)   the state of being a woman _____
ii) the state of being a man not a boy _____
iii) having the qualities of a woman _____
iv) having the qualities of a man _____

2 Place the following words in the right category. Ensure they fit with the theme and the context presented in the titles for each group.

juvenile   monogamy   triplets   married   mate   colleague   descendant
chum   quadruplets   comrade   bigamy   ally   stepfather   filial
accomplice   foster parents   in-law   bachelor   engaged   divorced

relationship status and marital status	relatives and family members	informal relationships	multiple births

3 These quotes are about social relationships. Share, think about, and discuss these quotes with your classmates.

"Each day of our lives we make deposits in the memory banks of our children."
Charles Swindoll

"Ultimately the bond of all companionship, whether in marriage or in friendship, is conversation."
Oscar Wilde

resident (noun)
Person who lives in a home or a particular place, as part of a community.
Residents feel the benefits of companionship and social interaction by living as part of this tight-knit community.

communal (adj)
Something belonging to or used by members of a group.
The communal pitch fell into disrepair during the pandemic.

suburb (noun)
An area on the periphery of the city where people who work in it reside.
Most of the factory workers live in the nearby suburbs.

ghetto (noun)
A low-income area of a city where various ethnic or religious groups tend to reside. Note: the plural form is irregular: ghettoes.
The ghetto may not be the nicest part of the city, but it has some of the nicest people I've ever met in my life.

town (noun)
An area where people live, work, and entertain themselves. Includes houses, commercial buildings, schools, etc, but it's smaller than a city.
Our town's main square has stood pristine for a hundred years, our residents take pride in keeping it like that for future generations to admire.

village (noun)
A grouping of housing and other buildings usually located in the countryside, smaller than a town.
There was a very small village not far from town where the residents hosted a communal market that we loved to visit every weekend.

hamlet (noun)
A very small village.
There was a lovely little hamlet at the foot of the mountain with a few residents living there.

borough (noun)
A section of a large town, usually with its own local government.
Many different boroughs made up the town, making it as diverse as its residents.

district (noun)
Area of a country or town with clearly defined borders used for business, political, educational, or any other special reason.
District four hasn't finished voting yet, the election hinges on their results!

slum (noun)
An overcrowded, low-income area with poor quality or self-made houses.
The slums wouldn't be in such a deplorable state if the government took immediate action.

neighbourhood (noun)
The immediate area surrounding where a person lives.
She loved living in the suburbs because it was a much quieter neighbourhood than the city.

colony (noun)
A country or area that is governed by another, usually larger, country.
As globalization continues to increase, it can be seen that there are strong trade links between countries and their former colonies.

citizen (noun)
Person who lives in a particular place who is awarded rights for being born there or for having lived there for some time.
When they wanted to hold him in the airport, he demanded his rights as a citizen be respected!

civil (adj)
Related to the population of a country and not to other organizations such as the military.
The civil rights movement saw people of all walks of life come together to demand justice in troubled times.

collective (noun)
Organization or business managed by the people who work in it and own it.
Our town's most beloved collective decided to start a new project in a nearby hamlet.

citizenship (noun)
Having legal rights and obligations by being a member of a country.
After many years of working tirelessly for the community, even though he was an immigrant, he was awarded citizenship by the mayor, in recognition of his contributions.

multi-ethnic (adj)
In relation to various different races.
The multi-ethnic communities of the borough's slums were very proud of their traditions.

affiliation (noun)
A liking for a particular group or thing.
There has always been a mutual affiliation between the football team and the local community.

service (noun)	Something someone does that is helpful, or valuable to others.
	Volunteer organizations are an essential part of the community because they provide valuable services to society such as keeping our beaches clean.
contribution (noun)	Something you can give to help make something successful.
	Their latest contribution was held in high regard by the residents of the town, who were grateful to the non-profit organization for their efforts.
to feel (a) part of (something) (verb)	To feel included or as if you belong (to something).
	We all like to feel part of a community, so when the neighbourhood set up a local charity to support the unemployed, she was delighted to help the other residents.
to be ostracized from (something) (verb)	To be excluded (from something) or ignored usually through deliberate unfriendly acts or through discrimination.
	The homeless are often said to be ostracized from society, yet this ostracism makes it even more difficult for them to reintegrate into the community.

Vocabulary practice

1   Find the odd one out in each of these groups of words.

i)   band, company, party, senate

ii)   government, settlement, congress, parliament

iii)   district, citizen, urban area, ghetto

iv)   gang, band, set, civil

2   Choose an adjective on the left to describe each word on the right.

humble	i) _____	suburb
hospitable	ii) _____	settlement
rustic	iii) _____	volunteer
picturesque	iv) _____	affiliation
helpful	v) _____	borough
impeccable	vi) _____	service

3   Explore and enjoy. Read, think about, and discuss these articles with your classmates.

THE IMPORTANCE OF COMMUNITY

Justine Clarabut

www.wellbeingpeople.com, 23rd July 2020

Researchers identify social factors inoculating some communities against coronavirus

Christopher Ingram

The Washington Post, 11th February 2021

C Social engagement

to be engaged in/on (something) (verb)

To be doing or involved in doing something.

He was so engaged in his charitable work that he was always busy doing something to help the local community.

engagement (noun)

Involvement in something.

Through social engagement, students can hope to expand their cultural experience through different interactions.

activism (noun)

Very specific and noticeable actions to achieve a result.

Environmental activism has been on the rise due to global demands to prevent climate change and the continuous degradation of our planet.

supporter (noun)

Individual who believes in a particular idea, group, or person.

Through her constant engagement with different organizations, she ended up becoming a strong supporter, dedicated to protecting wildlife.

the right to vote (noun)

To be allowed or entitled to vote (or express your preference for a political party or person) – usually formally in a national or local government election.

Some women were given the right to vote as long ago as 1902 in Australia, although universal suffrage was not accorded to Indigenous women, who had to wait another 60 years.

universal suffrage (noun)

Suffrage is the right to vote for people of a nation or state, so universal suffrage refers to that right being extended to all voting adults (eg at the age of 18 in the UK).

Despite universal suffrage being widely available, many are still fighting for equality.

to volunteer (verb), **volunteer** (noun)

To actively help with a cause or a concern in a practical way, without being asked or forced to do so.

After volunteering at a refugee camp, she became a supporter of worldwide care for displaced people around the globe.

A person who helps a cause or a concern in a practical way without charging money for their time.

In her spare time, she was a volunteer at the local old people's home, reading newspapers and playing card games with the residents.

charity (noun)

An organization which seeks to collect money or aid on behalf of those who may need it, eg those who are poor, unwell, or challenged in other ways.

As part of CAS, I regularly help my local charity to distribute food at the food bank.

charity work (noun)

Work or efforts made to support the work of an organization which helps others, without being paid for this work. (Usually British English.)

I spent the summer doing charity work at a local nursing home.

congregation (noun)

A gathering of people for religious purposes.

Volunteering to support those in need is one of the pillars and guiding principles of our congregation.

obligation (noun)

Something that someone feels they must do.

She felt a very strong obligation to take action, in an act of defiance against the unsavoury practices of the government in recent years.

enterprising (adj)

Something that is innovative and/or creative.

Her idea was very enterprising and as such was a huge success in reality.

social enterprise (noun)

A business organization which works for the benefit of society or to support a charity. A social enterprise would seek to make a profit but use that profit for charitable purposes. (Usually British English.)

Social enterprises seek to make the world a better place, like the Big Issue – a printed newspaper set up to help homeless people and one of the oldest and biggest social enterprises in the UK.

venture (noun)

A new activity or business that is accompanied by risk and uncertainty.

His new venture consisted of selling essential products at low cost, in order to help developing communities.

involvement (noun)

Being part of something.

Their involvement in that new venture was mired in uncertainty, but they knew that, together, they could tackle this enterprise through skill and determination.

to pledge (verb), **pledge** (noun)

A promise to take action.

Due to her untarnished record, she decided to pledge herself to the cause, and ensure that we get more vaccines to combat the pandemic, within the month.

to aid (verb)

To help or support.

The government influenced legislation in order to be able to aid those small businesses who suffered the worst during the pandemic.

to comfort (verb)

To help someone feel better when they're worried, sad or unwell.

He was comforted by the notion that help would arrive soon, regardless of what others said.

acceptance (noun)

To accept a difficult or unpleasant situation.

Our derided acceptance of the events proves once again that people with bad intentions can corrupt even the noblest of goals.

commission (noun)

A request to do a certain piece of work.

She was contacted to work on a commission focusing on globalization, so she got to work on writing her article.

to advocate (verb), **advocate** (noun), **advocacy** (noun)

To support, recommend or promote a plan, idea or procedure. A supporter of a plan, idea or procedure. Support for a plan, idea or procedure.

The professor was well known for advocating human rights since the 1980's.

She was an advocate for women's rights throughout her career.

By being part of the "Environmental Awareness Advocacy Movement", he made sure to always be willing to explain his ideas to any passer-by.

militant (adj)

A determined, active individual willing to use force, if necessary.

Militant groups decided to storm the national museum and cause mayhem as an act of defiance against the government's new policies. It saddens me to think that they believe damaging our shared heritage will get them our support.

to protest (verb)

To strongly complain in disagreement or opposition to something.

The group decided to protest in front of congress, despite the restrictions imposed on public demonstrations earlier that month.

to take action (verb)

To become more active, possibly for a political or charitable cause.

Rather than sitting at home, I decided to take action and start campaigning for a more sustainable lifestyle.

to get (*or* be) involved (in something) (verb)

To take part in an activity or give an activity (or cause) your time, hard work, and attention.

When my Diploma studies are complete and I have a bit more time to myself, I hope to get involved in more volunteering.

petition (noun)

A formal document signed by a group of people or a community to call for a government or other official organization to do something they believe is important or necessary.

More than 5000 people in the peace demonstration signed an anti-war petition asking the government to pull out troops from the warzone.

to take to the streets (verb)

To gather with other people on the street of a town or community in order to celebrate an event or to show that you disagree with or oppose something.

The right to protest is not a universal right across all countries, so some people never take to the streets to show their opposition to government.

demonstration (noun)

Event in which people march in favour or against, something or someone.

Last week's gathering was a demonstration unlike any other in support of the brave firefighters who risked everything to save those in need.

picket (noun), **to picket** (verb)

An event in which workers bar entry to an area or place, as a sign of protest.

Factory workers were advised to return home and cease their protest, after being reminded of the new laws against picketing.

to strike (verb)	To stop working as a sign of protest against unfavourable working conditions, salary disputes, etc.
	Migrant workers decided to go on strike after they realized that their wages were dismal compared to others in the industry.
to boycott (verb)	To refuse to participate in an activity or buy a particular product to express disapproval.
	The starlet decided to boycott that brand of make-up, and so she stopped using it on her streams and video blogs, after allegations of animal testing and cruelty were made against that company.

Vocabulary practice

1 **Find as many different verbs as you can that collocate with each noun in the table. (One has been done for you as an example.)**

Noun	Verbs
pledge	*to make a pledge*
advocacy	
engagement	
involvement	
congregation	
obligation	

2 **Word transformation. Transform these words into nouns (*or* doers of the actions). Choose the correct suffix: *-er*, *-or*, *-neur*. (Note that *one* of these words takes no suffix and does not change.)**

i) picketing _____

ii) demonstration _____

iii) protest _____

iv) commission _____

v) enterprise _____

vi) venture _____

vii) advocate _____

3 **Explore and enjoy. Read this article. Then discuss your thoughts on it with a classmate.**

"Why social engagement is so important for all of us"

Peter Hatherley Green

thenationalnews.com

college (noun)
A place of higher education and/or professional development. (May also be a secondary school in the UK.)
After graduating high school, I plan to go to college abroad!

pedagogy (noun)
Field of study that focuses on the profession of teaching, its methods, and its practice.
The teacher's pedagogy was challenged by the headteacher for its unorthodox style.

vocational (adj)
Providing the necessary skills or tools needed in preparation to carry out a particular job.
The vocational counsellor ensured that his students were prepared for the challenges of an international university application process.

credentials (noun)
All the background information pertaining to someone's level of skill and experience and/or expertise.
Her credentials showed that she was perfect for the job!

qualifications (noun)
The educational or training examinations you have successfully passed so that you can enter a specific course, job, or profession.
Eloise always wanted to study medicine. She worked hard for her IB Diploma but needed more qualifications before she could work as a doctor.

academic (adj)
Relating to education and knowledge.
The academic board decided that the inclusion of vocational activities into the curriculum was now mandatory.

literate (adj), **literacy** (noun)
The ability to read and write. (The opposite of literate is illiterate.)
Whilst the global literacy rate has increased over the years, only 86% of the world's population are literate.

(to gain) a scholarship (verb)
To have your studies paid for either by the college or university you attend or by another organization.
I will work hard to gain a scholarship from a well-known business school which awards scholarships to top IB Diploma graduates.

to apply for a grant (verb)
A grant is an amount of money given by an organization usually for a specific purpose (e.g. to buy a computer, to pay for your education, or to pay for repairs to your home). If you apply for a grant, you make a formal request for this amount of money.
My mother has financial problems caused by her unemployment, so I hope to apply for a grant to help pay for my studies.

gap year (noun)
A period of time taken out of studies to go travelling and/or to take up voluntary work, or to gain essential work experience. It usually describes a break of one year after finishing school and before starting at college or university.
I plan to take a gap year and travel round Europe before starting my degree.

remote learning (noun)
Where your education or lessons take place outside of a usual classroom situation, and not in the same place or room as your teacher. (Also known as distance learning.)
Because of the pandemic schools had to move to remote learning, since face-to-face teaching was temporarily banned.

independent learning (noun)
Where a student takes responsibility for their own learning, makes good decisions about organizing their time and studies, with less frequent support and guidance from the teacher.
Independent learning and the organizational and study skills it requires will be key to your success as an undergraduate student.

method (noun)
A specific manner of doing something.
A unified academic method of instruction was proposed by the board, although a lot of teachers felt slighted by the lack of independence this would bring to their lessons.

didactic (adj)

Something designed with the intent to teach.

The students proposed a variety of didactic activities to promote the joy of reading for kindergarten children.

autodidactic (adj)

Being able to learn on one's own without a teacher.

She turned out to be an autodidactic young learner who learned to write in cursive all on her own.

tuition (noun)

Teaching or instruction, usually in a specific subject.

Some students choose to pay for private tuition in Maths to try and improve their grade.

tuition (fees) (noun)

Money paid in order to receive an education in a college or university.

She decided to work on a summer job to help her parents pay her tuition (fees).

to mentor (verb)

To provide recurrent advice to another who is younger and inexperienced.

As a caring teacher, he made sure to always mentor his young students, and be ready to lend a hand.

tutor (noun)

A teacher who helps students with specific academic needs, for various or specific subjects.

As a tutor, she was in charge of a group of students who tended to get into a lot of trouble.

to counsel (verb)

To provide advice on various issues.

As an experienced mentor, she always tried to counsel students on the best course of action.

council (noun)

A group of individuals in charge of making official decisions or advising others.

To ensure order and proper engagement of the students has been one of the main objectives of this year's student council.

curriculum (noun)

Compendium of subjects and all their contents, to be studied in any institution dedicated to learning.

That subject's curriculum was too hard for the students to follow.

extracurricular (adj)

Activity or subject outside of the regular curriculum.

Her extracurricular activities included football and fencing!

honours (noun)

Awarded recognition that receives high praise and respect.

When she graduated with honours, all her fellow students stood up and cheered in recognition of her accomplishments.

attainment (noun)

Something that is achieved.

You need to work hard in your subjects to reach the desired level of attainment your parents expect.

refinement (noun)

Working at something to make it better.

Your language skills will require some refinement before you can take the international examinations.

sorority (noun)

In the United States, a sorority is an exclusive club or society for females at a university.

Mia liked being part of the sorority because she enjoyed organising events for them.

fraternity (noun)

In the United States, a fraternity is an exclusive club or society for males at a university.

Boys in the fraternity meet at weekends to socialize and do sports.

1 **The following groups of words make quotations. Try to put the words in order, experiment with them to make a sentence. Then look them up online to check.**

    i)   opens / closes / a / a / he / school / prison / door / who
           Victor Hugo

    ii)   survives / learned / forgotten / been / has / has / been / what / when / education / is / what
           B F Skinner

    iii) violence / vaccine / education / the / is / for
           E J Olmos

2 **Explore and enjoy. Read, think, and discuss this article with your classmates.**

    Career choices in a post-pandemic world
    The Times of India, 27th April 2021

3 **Explore and enjoy. Listen to this podcast. Then discuss your thoughts on it with a classmate. Do you think schools with no rules really are the future?**

Future Proofing Our Schools
BBC Radio 4
24th March 2021

colleagues (noun)
Individuals who share a workplace or work together often.
It's good to know I can reach out to my colleagues for advice.

assistant (noun)
Someone who helps another person with various tasks.
I'd be lost without my assistant!

supervisor (noun)
Someone whose job is to oversee the activities of others.
His supervisor got very angry at him for being late again.

executive (noun)
A high-ranking businessperson who is part of the decision-making structure.
Even as a high-ranking executive, he still has lunch with the regular staff members and always treats them as equals.

CEO (chief executive officer) (noun)
Highest position in a company.
She was named the new CEO of the company, even though she is still very young.

project (noun)
A planned activity with a particular method and objective.
The new building project came in under budget and was still completed ahead of schedule.

job prospects (noun)
Prospects are the chance or possibility of success, so job prospects refer to the likelihood of securing paid work.
The COVID-19 pandemic has had a huge impact on the availability of work, so job prospects are poor.

public sector (noun)
The part of a nation's economy where the government (or public money) pays the salaries and for the running of the organization, usually education, emergency healthcare, the road network, etc.
Some people choose to work in the public sector because they know their contribution will have a direct benefit to society.

private sector (noun)
The part of a nation's economy where the businesses and industry are not owned by the government but by private individuals or groups of individuals.
Statistics show that the private sector provides about 80% of the workforce with employment in the UK.

employment (noun)
Being paid to do a job at a specific workplace.
Looking for employment has become quite a challenge during the pandemic.

self-employment (noun)
Where you work for yourself. A self-employed person is not paid a regular salary by another person or business but is paid for the services they provide and arranges for their own taxes to be paid, etc.
Self-employment where you are your own boss is very attractive, but there are also risks.

unemployment (noun)
Not having a job or source of income.
Unemployment rates are at an all-time low! People are very happy with the new government policies.

full-time employment (noun)
Paid work where you work for the whole of the usual working week.
After I have left university, I hope to find full-time employment in the public sector.

part-time employment (noun)
Paid work where you work for some of the usual working week (e.g. three days or every evening), and less than someone in full-time employment.
Even though I'm studying, I still need to find part-time employment to earn some money.

annual leave (noun)
'Leave' means the days you are allowed to take as holiday (in the UK) or vacation (in the US) where your employer still pays you. So annual leave is the number of days in one year.
He gets 25 days of annual leave, and usually spends most of this time on holiday in his home country.

to be made redundant (verb), **redundancy** (noun)
To be asked to leave your work, because your job is no longer needed, or the company is closing down so your salary cannot be paid. (In the US, 'to be dismissed'.)
Many people were made redundant as rapid advances were made in digital technology.

to resign (verb), **resignation** (noun)
To choose to leave a job and formally state you are leaving.
I will resign from my part-time job here when I leave to go to university.

trainee (noun), **to train** (verb)
Someone who is employed to learn the basic skills of the job; they are learning how to do a specific role.
As a graduate trainee, you are part of a programme where you work in each department of the bank.

apprenticeship, apprentice (noun)
Period of learning the intricacies of a job and the skills needed, under the tutelage of another. A person being taught the specific skills for a job.
She spent her apprenticeship period learning from one of the company's most successful salesmen!
After a year as an apprentice, she was ready to take the practical mechanic's exam.

internship, intern (noun)
Period of learning the intricacies of a job, the skill needed, and training.
A person learning the specific skills for a job through experience.
During my internship, I learned some valuable lessons you can't find in a textbook.
She thought she'd be in with a good chance of getting the job, especially since she'd been an intern at the company.

coaching (noun)
Training or aid in a specific subject.
Through proper coaching, he was able to get the promotion he wanted.

performance (noun)
How well an action is carried out in a specific field.
His performance review was satisfactory, but he still needs to improve a lot if he's hoping for a promotion this year.

promotion (noun)
Award of a higher rank or position.
After working so hard for many years, he finally got that promotion he was waiting for.

demotion (noun)
Going down to a lower rank or position.
The boss gave him a demotion when he found out he had been leaving work early each day for months.

probationary period (noun)
After starting a new job, the period of time where your employer decides whether you are suited to the work and where you are allowed formally to continue in the role.
Once her probationary period was complete, she felt able to put a deposit on a new car and drive to work, and not take public transport.

tenure (noun)
When a job is made permanent. Most common in the US.
After many years of hard work, my history teacher got tenure, which is a load off his mind.

mediation (noun)
Helping two sides come together for an agreement and resolve their issues.
After several rounds of negotiation, his mediation proved effective to ensure the contract was signed.

efficiency (noun)
Energy and time well spent without waste.
She had reached peak efficiency in her role, which is why she got promoted so early.

procrastination (noun)
Delay completing something, often due to the boring nature of it.
Procrastination during work hours is one clear sign of an unmotivated workforce.

qualifications (noun)
Levels of skill and experience required to perform a job or action.
With her excellent qualifications and her exceptional internship, she was able to procure gainful employment with our company.

attributes (noun)
Someone's qualities, character, or characteristics.
Some of his greatest attributes were nourished during his apprenticeship.

professional (adj)
Someone that has had special education and specific training to be able to do something.
After years of training, she was proud to say she was finally a professional accountant.

experienced (adj)
Someone who has knowledge and skill acquired by doing something many times.
As an experienced programmer, he knows when our systems need a security update.

licensed (adj)	Officially allowed to do, sell, or have something.
	An "officially licensed product" is not always of the highest quality.
competent (adj)	Able to do something properly.
	Throughout her internship, she was competent enough to be considered for future employment, sooner than expected.
competitive (adj)	Products, services, etc, that are as good or better than others.
	Their flagship product was not very competitive in the market, its price was simply too steep.

Vocabulary practice

1   **Match the idioms with their explanations.**

i)	dead-end job	end of a contract
ii)	glass ceiling	no opportunity to be promoted
iii)	laid off	to do just what is expected
iv)	nine to five	office work
v)	work to rule	an invisible barrier to achieve a promotion

2   **Explore and enjoy. Read, think about, and discuss this article with your classmates.**

"Enhancing worker productivity': Joe Biden signs minimum wage boost for federal contract employees"

Josh Boak

The Sydney Morning Herald, 28th April 2021

Social Organization

F Law and order

lawful (adj)
Something that is permitted by law.
After becoming his lawful heir, he was also welcomed to live with his new family.

lawless (adj)
Something that is not overseen or controlled by law.
The frontier was a lawless land without a hint of justice.

crime (noun), **criminal** (adj)
Something illegal; relating to illegal activities.
After his last criminal offence, he was tried and prosecuted for various terrible crimes.

to break the law (verb)
Here, 'the law' refers to a group or system of legal rules which a society considers necessary in order to manage crime and ensure all people can live and work safely. If you 'break the law', you commit a crime or take part in criminal behaviour which goes against this legal set of rules.
As insurance costs rise, more drivers are tempted to break the law and drive irresponsibly without car insurance.

to commit an offence (verb)
If you commit a crime or a sin, you do something bad or illegal. An offence is usually a specific crime or wrongdoing. If you commit an offence against the law, you will be punished. (See **minor offence**.)
He admitted that he was there at the time but strongly denied having committed any offence.

minor offence (UK) (*or* **offense (US)**) (noun)
Bad behaviour or illegal activities which are relatively small and less serious when compared to other crimes or offences.
The police would not prosecute for some minor offences, but would give a caution, particularly for a first-time offender.

shoplifting (noun)
The act of taking items from a shop when it is open but without paying for them, usually hiding the items in your bag or under clothing.
Shoplifting as a crime results in significant costs for the legal system, for the shops, but also for society as a whole.

identity theft (noun)
The crime of getting personal information about someone else usually without them knowing or knowingly giving their permission – often to obtain money or to gain access to their bank account.
The bank always tells us never to give anyone your bank card or password information to avoid any opportunity for identity theft.

domestic violence (noun)
Aggressive behaviour or acts which take place at your home, usually at the hands of someone you know.
We often think of domestic violence as violence against women, but increasingly men are victims, too.

sexual harassment (noun)
Unwelcome, inappropriate, and very often repeated behaviour which may include comments, jokes, or physical contact which are sexual in nature. It often refers specifically to the workplace, although may occur somewhere else as well.
Whilst social media has done a great deal to publicize the #MeToo movement, many social media influencers still find themselves victims of sexual harassment online.

justice (noun)
Quality of being fair and impartial.
Justice was served after the trial against the animal abuser.

judiciary (noun)
A government branch designed to handle a country's legal system.
Members of the judiciary encouraged the population to participate in the public opinion polls for the new law.

jury, juror (noun)
In a court, the group of ordinary people chosen from the general public who are presented with the facts about a crime and then decide if they believe someone is guilty (ie they have committed the crime) or not guilty (ie they are innocent of the crime).
Twelve jurors decided the fate of the woman accused of that horrible crime.

to prosecute (verb), **prosecution** (noun)

To put a person accused of committing an illegal act or crime on trial in a court. The process of carrying out a trial in court with the intent of proving the guilt of the accused.

Everyone agreed there was more than sufficient evidence to prosecute both of them for the robbery.

The trial ended with a successful prosecution. Both defendants were found guilty.

defendant (noun)

The person accused of a crime in a court of law who has to defend themselves, presenting evidence to support their case.

At the end of the long trial, the defendant was found guilty.

to testify (verb)

To make a statement under oath during a trial in court.

He was willing to testify against his abuser, but only if they could ensure his safety.

verdict (noun)

Decision reached after all facts have been brought to light and all parties involved have presented their cases in a court of law.

After all his unlawful schemes came to light, the verdict was unequivocally 'guilty'.

prison (noun)

A building where criminals are held once they are found guilty of a crime, or where people go whilst they wait for their trial to take place.

Mr Nelson Mandela walked free from prison in 1990 after being locked up for 27 years.

imprisonment (noun)

When a person is detained in a secure location such as a prison after being found guilty of a crime.

He was sentenced to life imprisonment for his crimes.

sentence (noun)

The formal punishment that you are given as a result of being found guilty of a crime in a court of law.

The judge handed him a two-year sentence in prison.

community service (noun)

A punishment where you are told to carry out unpaid work which will benefit society and is often seen as a way to put right what you have done. You would be given this punishment instead of going to prison.

The community service involved him clearing away rubbish and cleaning graffiti from the school walls.

electronic tag (UK) *or* **monitor (US)** (noun)

An electronic device placed on the ankle or sometimes the wrist to monitor the movements of someone. This can be used as an alternative to imprisonment or to prevent antisocial behaviour.

An electronic monitor can be used as a sentence for crimes or more recently has been used for making sure individuals stay in home quarantine.

to pay one's debt to society (verb)

An idiom which describes how you have completed the requirements of the sentence you were given for the crime (e.g. completed your time in prison, paid any fines, or carried out community service).

Once he'd completed his five years in prison, he said he'd paid his debt to society and should no longer be considered a criminal.

indictment (noun)

Official statement accusing someone of an offence.

The businessman was fired after he was arrested on an indictment of fraud against the company.

case (noun)

A situation required to be investigated or considered by the police or a court of law.

The case was handled with much scrutiny, to ensure no evidence went overlooked.

precedent (noun)

A previous decision, that can be used as the basis to resolve a similar case.

As there was no precedent for a case like this one, the judge had a very tough verdict to pass.

legislation (noun)

Law, or a set of laws, proposed by a governmental organism.

The proposed legislation will aim to tackle some very controversial issues.

regulation (noun)

An official rule.

The regulations must be upheld if we hope to properly combat the virus and stay safe.

implementation (noun)

When an established norm, mandate, system, etc. begins to be used.

The new law's abrupt implementation was met with a lot of scepticism from the population.

to ratify (verb)	To officially approve new legislation.	
	People celebrated on the streets after the new labour law was ratified.	

clause (noun) — A particular section of a written legal document.
A single clause in the contract she forgot to read is now the cause of her crippling debt.

amendment (noun) — A change made to a law that has not gone into effect yet.
The last amendment to be made to the new legislation was met with so much backlash, the government had to go back to square one.

code (noun) — A set of principles agreed upon and used by societies, organizations, groups, etc.
Our moral code forbids such appalling actions to take place in public.

constitution (noun) — The compendium of laws and principles that govern a country.
We are protected under the laws of our constitution, so we will never stop fighting for justice!

summons (noun) — A requirement to appear in a court of law.
The multinational's company representative was sent to answer the supreme court's summons.

warrant (noun) — An official document that enables the police to search a home, make arrests, etc.
The police had a search warrant to check every inch of the house, they were quite surprised when they found a large cache of illegal goods.

Vocabulary practice

1 Match the adjectives on the left to the nouns on the right to make as many different descriptions as you can.

	Adjectives	Nouns
i)	solitary	law
ii)	common	criminal
iii)	good	confinement
iv)	petty	cause
v)	probable	conduct

2 Find the correct preposition to complete the synonyms of the following verbs.

up   out   up   with

	Verb		Synonym	Preposition
i)	support	=	back	_____
ii)	escape without punishment	=	get away	_____
iii)	solve, resolve	=	clear	_____
iv)	choose, select	=	pick	_____

3 Explore and enjoy. Read, think, and discuss this article with your classmates.

DeSantis signs 'anti-mob' legislation into law in response to George Floyd protests
Ana Ceballos
Miami Herald, 19th April 2021

Sharing the planet

A The environment

ecology (noun)
The scientific study of the relationship between land, water, animals, air, etc.
She decided that studying an 'ecology-based' major would help the planet more than just protesting against climate change.

to recycle (verb)
To produce something useful out of materials that are now trash. (See **to upcycle**.)
We need to encourage people to recycle their waste to foster a more sustainable lifestyle.

to upcycle (verb)
To repair, adapt, and improve an old item (eg clothing, furniture) that would otherwise be waste material. (See **to recycle**.)
While recycling might be very practical, upcycling is usually very creative and by reusing items we ensure fewer emissions are produced, so the environment benefits even more.

to reuse (verb)
To use something more than once or for a new purpose.
If we focused more on reusing old things, we could generate less waste and conserve natural resources.

natural resources (noun)
Things that are found on planet earth and that humans use.
If we don't make changes to our choices and lifestyles, many natural resources could be depleted in the near future.

conservation (noun/adj)
Care and protection of the environment, or particular ecological or ancient sites for posterity.
Conservation of the nature reserve by locals means it is now thriving.

preservation (noun)
Care and protection of something.
The preservation of historical places is important so that they can still be enjoyed by future generations.

sustainable (adj)
Able to be maintained through the passing of time with very little or no effect on the environment.
In order to shift to a more sustainable method of energy production, we need to heavily invest in advanced technology.

renewable (adj)
Energy forms which can be replaced almost as quickly as they are used.
One of the biggest reasons why we haven't fully shifted to renewable energy is the costs in comparison to using fossil fuels, which are cheaper.

global warming (noun)
The gradual increase in temperature of the earth's atmosphere over many years as a result of human activity (eg the burning of fossil fuels) which creates gases and high levels of carbon dioxide.
Scientists believe that global warming is leading to more incidents of extreme weather, for example unexpected drought, severe rain and flooding, as well as hurricanes.

greenhouse gases (noun)
Gases in the earth's atmosphere which allow sunlight in but prevent heat from leaving. These include water vapour, carbon dioxide, methane, and ozone.
Of course, greenhouse gases are good in some ways – but you can have too much of a good thing and scientists worry that our activities are adding too much to these gases.

carbon emissions (noun)
The carbon dioxide that human activity (such as factories, aeroplanes, and cars) produces which is released into the atmosphere and harms the environment.
For the last ten years now, the UK's carbon emissions have fallen significantly, largely as a result of closing power plants which burn fossil fuel.

carbon footprint (noun)
A measurement of the amount of carbon emissions that an activity, an individual, or group of individuals (eg company, country, industry) releases into the earth's atmosphere over a period of time.
We all have to do our bit to reduce our carbon footprint, and I will try to cycle to school rather than ask my Dad to drive me in the car.

endangered (adj)
Under threat of disappearing or becoming extinct.
Today, there is a growing number of endangered species thanks to human activities.

pollution (noun)

Damage caused to the environment as a result of human activities.

Pollution affects people as much as it does the environment, yet we still shy away from renewable energy sources.

deforestation (noun)

The process of cutting down vast numbers of trees in places such as the Amazon Rainforest.

Due to deforestation, many endangered animals are now also losing their homes.

energy (noun)

Power generated from something like water, air, electricity, etc.

Nuclear energy can outperform any other alternative, but the risks that come with it can be very high.

toxic (adj)

Harmful, poisonous.

Toxic frogs use bright colours to signal a warning to any would-be predators.

waste (noun)

Things that are thrown away or are left over after a process.

As domestic waste continues to pile up, more people are at risk of disease.

hazard (noun)

Something that presents a risk of being dangerous and/or harmful.

The level of pollution in some countries has resulted in various, health-related, hazards for its residents.

fracking (noun)

The process of cracking rocks deep under the earth to collect natural gas.

Uncontrolled fracking can result in catastrophic issues for the environment.

desertification (noun)

The process in which soil becomes dry and barren, often because of over farming or human activities.

Large parts of the area are at risk of desertification if farming practices don't change soon.

scarcity (noun)

An acute lack of something which becomes very hard to find.

As a result of desertification in the countryside, people have had to face food scarcity and hunger.

industrialization (noun)

The growth of manufacturing and production in a country.

The rapid industrialization of our country has brought economic growth at the cost of many fragile environments.

prevention (noun)

The process of taking precautions to stop something from happening.

Through active prevention and strong government backing, park rangers have been able to significantly reduce the illegal hunting of endangered species.

impact (noun)

A strong effect something has on others which can be positive or negative.

Human activity has generated an irreparable impact on our environments.

ecosystem (noun)

A group of living organisms living in conjunction with each other, forming an interdependent cycle.

Even though pests can be a hassle, they play a crucial role in the ecosystem.

habitat (noun)

Natural environment in which living organisms live.

Endangered species are slowly going back to their natural habitat, to begin to the arduous process of becoming strong communities once more,

biodiversity (noun)

The variety of organisms that live in a specific area.

Preserving and ensuring biodiversity is what keeps our ecosystems vibrant and teeming with life.

bioscience (noun)

The study of living things.

In bioscience, all life matters, even insects and plants.

wildlife (noun)

Animals and plants that live independently in areas with no people, under natural conditions.

Some areas teeming with wildlife have come under threat due to widespread deforestation.

forestry (noun)

The study and preservation of woodland areas.

Preserving our woodlands is one of the main mandates of those who undertake the challenges of dedicating their time to forestry.

1 Match the environmental problems on the left to solutions on the right.

i) deforestation	reduce, reuse, and recycle
ii) fumes, gas emissions	respect, protect, preserve the ecosystem
iii) loss of biodiversity	conservation
iv) endangered species	clean power
v) degraded environments	preservation of the natural world
vi) consumerism	protection of habitats

2 Complete the idioms with one of the following words. (First try, then search online and/or ask your teacher.)

woods	fresh	fuel	rainbows	flames
ground	rains	wood	green	grass

i) to have _____ fingers

ii) to let the _____ grow under your feet

iii) fan the _____

iv) when it _____ , it pours

v) chase _____

vi) to add _____ to the fire

vii) to be out of the _____

viii) a breath of _____ air

ix) can't see the _____ for the trees

x) to gain _____

3 Explore and enjoy. Share, discuss, and think about this article with your classmates:

"For #EarthDay, 7 Famous Environmental Speeches By Women"
denisegraveline.org, 17th April 2015

B Human rights

morality (noun)
Judgement or belief about whether behaviour is right or wrong.
When people do unspeakable things, their morality always comes into question.

immoral (adj)
Outside of societal expectations and standards.
His immoral behaviour got him kicked out of the church.

stereotype (noun)
An assumption about the qualities or features of someone based on generalized beliefs, which are usually wrong.
Stereotypes can cause discrimination and segregation amongst communities.

discrimination (noun)
The treatment of individuals differently, usually badly, based on their race, age, gender, etc.
Whenever a minority is treated unfairly, discrimination allegations soon follow.

minorities (noun)
Small groups in society who are different from others, based on their race, religion, beliefs, etc.
Some minorities face unjust discrimination from dominant groups in society.

segregation (noun)
Keeping people separated from others and treating them differently, usually badly, based on their race, age, gender, origin, etc.
Segregating people under false pretences or ignorant notions is truly the lowest human beings have gone.

freedom of expression (noun)
The act of demonstrating a feeling, idea or emotion, verbally or physically.
Freedom of expression cannot occur when the government controls or silences the media.

repression (noun)
Using force or violence to pacify and/or control a group of individuals.
The government cracked down on protesters yesterday, in another show of brutal repression against those who oppose them.

suppression (noun)
The prevention of something from being known or expressed.
The suppression of information on the subject has left a lot of people wondering what happened after the plane crash.

violation (noun)
Something that breaks a law, agreement, right, etc.
Preventing children from going to school is a violation of their human rights.

right (noun)
Something that all people are entitled to do or have by law. Rights can also apply to animals.
All children have the right to be educated.

Universal Declaration of Human Rights (noun)
The Universal Declaration of Human Rights is an international document drawn up by the United Nations with the support of the international community which seeks to summarize the basic human rights of all individuals. This includes the right to education, or the right to a nationality.

amnesty (noun)
1 Decision by a government to forgive a crime and avoid punishment for a crime committed.
The government has decided to grant amnesty to those illegal immigrants who voluntarily sign up for the citizenship process, regardless of how long they've been in the country illegally.
2 A period of time where a person can own up to doing something or hand in an illegal possession without fear of arrest.
The police have declared an amnesty on offensive weapons for the month of April. People are encouraged to take any sorts of knives, guns, or other weapons to their local police station for safe disposal.

politics (noun)
Actions and policies through which a country is governed.
Some people think that politics is a dirty business, but they might fail to realize that governments have to deal with the 'moral' and 'immoral' elements that make up our societies.

trafficking (noun)
The act of transporting, buying, or selling products illegally. Usually associated with drugs or illegal weapons.
Countries in conflict are often hotbeds for gun trafficking and worse…

human trafficking (noun)

The act of transporting, buying, or selling people illegally. This is often against the will of a person for example in the case of sex trafficking.

The United Nations has chosen 30th July each year to be seen as World Day Against Human Trafficking.

prostitution (noun)

The exchange of sexual acts for money. Prostitution is considered immoral in some cultures and is an illegal activity in some countries.

Impoverished areas can be rife with prostitution and drug trafficking where some people are pushed into these practices in order to survive.

slavery (noun)

When a human is said to be 'owned' by another and can be forced into any form of labour.

In some areas of the world, workers' wages are so low and working conditions so harsh, that it can be considered a form of modern slavery.

abuse (noun)

Verbal, emotional, physical, or financial mistreatment of another person or animal.

It's really important to offer support and friendship to people who are victims of abuse, and there are a number of charities that can help.

to abuse (verb)

To treat another person (or animal) in a terrible way, which can be a violent incident or can happen over a long period of time.

Those who abuse others are often the victims of abuse themselves in their earlier life.

to coerce (noun)

To force or manipulate someone into doing something they would otherwise not do.

Some people are coerced into trafficking illegal products and if they don't comply, they are threatened with abuse.

exploitation (noun)

The process of using or manipulating something or someone to gain an advantage or for your own gain.

Immigrant exploitation has become a serious issue in some parts of the world.

deportation (noun)

The process of forcing someone to leave a country for breaking the law, or because they were there illegally.

Some of the factory workers were faced with possible deportation for entering the country illegally.

humanitarian (adj)

Something intended to improve the lives of others and help them in order to reduce hardship.

Humanitarian aid is crucial in places where the pandemic has struck the hardest.

aid (noun)

Something given to those in need to help them in a practical way such as food, medicine, money, etc.

The government asked for aid from other countries to help them to recover from the floods.

humane (adj)

Something done with kindness and the intent of doing little or no harm to others.

The world is in dire need of more humane laws that protect those less fortunate.

inhumane (adj)

Something that is not done with kindness and can be cruel or cause harm to others.

The inhumane treatment of the refugees has caused widespread condemnation by people around the world.

tolerance (noun)

The acceptance and respect for the opinions or beliefs of others, without having to agree with them.

Through tolerance and understanding of others we have a chance to make the world a better place.

1 **These statements are taken from the Universal Declaration of Human Rights. Choose from the following words to complete the statements:**

entitled	**equal**
degrading	liberty
declaration	expression
everyone	**rights**
torture	security

    i)   All human beings are born free and _____ in dignity and _____ .

    ii)   Everyone is _____ to all the rights and freedoms set forth in this _____ .

    iii) Everyone has the right to life, _____ and _____ of person.

    iv) No one shall be subjected to _____ , or to cruel, inhuman or _____ treatment or punishment.

    v)   _____ has the right to freedom of opinion and _____ .

2 **Reorder these words to make famous quotations. Add suitable punctuation marks. Think about the meanings of the quotes and discuss your ideas with a partner.**

    i)   is / is / an / a / of / of / not / it / poverty / justice / act / overcoming / gesture / charity

         (*two sentences*)

         Nelson Mandela

    ii)   people / humanity / human / deny / is / to / to / very / rights / their / their / challenge

         Nelson Mandela

    iii) person / person / yourself / it / do / be / led / wait / don't / to / to

         Mother Teresa

    iv) hate / hate / love / that / do / can / out / drive / only / cannot

         Reverend Dr Martin Luther King Jnr

3 **Read the following article which summarizes ten examples of human rights. Add three more rights of your own then discuss your choices with your classmates.**

Ten examples of human rights

humanrightscareers.com

C Peace and conflict

accord (noun)
A formal agreement.
The ceasefire began immediately after both countries had signed the accord.

armistice (noun)
When two sides in a conflict agree to talk about ways to make peace instead of fighting.
People believed the end of the war was finally in sight when the countries agreed to an armistice.

treaty (noun)
A formal, written agreement between several states or countries.
The treaty of Versailles signalled the end of World War I.

pact (noun)
An informal, usually verbal, agreement between individuals or groups.
A pact between the rebel forces and the army has been reached, people are hopeful of possible disarmament to follow.

disarmament (noun)
The process of removing or reducing the number of weapons.
The rebel forces finally agreed to an armistice and gradual disarmament.

pacifism (noun)
The belief that conflict and warfare are wrong and should not occur.
Through pacifism, we have achieved great victories in the name of peace and prosperity.

cooperation (noun)
When people work together to reach a common goal.
A treaty promising cooperation and joint military operations was signed between the two countries to face the growing terrorist threat.

neutrality (noun), **neutral** (adj)
The quality or state of being independent and unbiased, usually in an argument, conflict or in wartime.
Switzerland is well-known for its neutrality, and even now, its foreign policy imposes the principle that it will not engage in any conflict with another state.

reunification (noun)
When previously separated sections of a country get together and become a whole country once more.
The road to reunification between north and south has been long and bloody, but thanks to the peacekeeping efforts of other countries, it's finally a reality.

peacekeeping (adj)
Something that helps to prevent conflict. Often refers to armed forces used as a visual deterrent in an area where there has been a conflict or unrest.
The peacekeeping force was called in to bring order to the troubled conflict zone.

serenity (noun)
The state of being at peace, calm, tranquil, etc.
After the armistice was signed, there was an unprecedented period of serenity on the front lines.

hostility (noun), **hostile** (adj)
Deliberate unfriendliness towards others.
As part of their attack, the army encouraged ongoing hostilities at the border.

war (noun)
A specific armed conflict between two opposing sides that happens over a significant period of time. Throughout history, significant wars are often named such as World War II.
The war between the two countries went on for five years.

(to be) at war (verb, idiom)
To be in a state of conflict or disagreement, or actively involved in armed conflict.
The two nations have been at war for some time, with lives lost on both sides.

warfare (noun)
The type of fighting that takes places within a war or conflict situation.
Rebel forces continue to engage in brutal warfare with the army.

cyberwarfare (noun)
Online sabotage such as deliberate transmission of a virus or hacking into systems owned by a rival, enemy, or other nation state.
Before the attack, their equipment malfunctioned due to deliberate sabotage, thanks to cyberwarfare operations carried out by our forces.

biological warfare (noun)
A type of warfare (or fighting) which makes use of viruses, poisons, or bacteria. (Also called biowarfare, or germ warfare.)
We think of biological warfare as modern, but early incidents may have involved arrowheads being stuck into the ground before use, so that the injuries they caused were more likely to be infected.

5 Sharing the planet

chemical warfare (noun)

A type of warfare (or fighting) which makes use of chemicals other than explosives (e.g. gases which can suffocate, burn skin, or damage nerves).

Because of the horrible experiences of the war, the international community banned the use of chemical weapons after World War 1, but I'm unsure whether this means we will always live in a world without chemical warfare.

weapons (noun)

Items that are designed purposefully to cause harm or kill such as various types of knives, guns, bombs, etc often used in times of war or conflict.

Both sides agreed to put down their weapons as a show of willingness to abide by the armistice.

warmonger (noun)

A leader who deliberately encourages their represented group or country to go to war without considering alternative options.

The prime minister was declared a 'warmonger', after the devastation the armed forces caused under his orders.

devastation (noun)

Extreme damage and destruction.

After the horrible devastation caused by the bombings, refugees headed in the thousands to the border checkpoints.

bombing (noun)

A deliberate attack on a place during a war or conflict, usually over a period of time using explosives, or a single explosive often thrown by a terrorist or suicide bomber.

Major cities across Europe suffered from regular bombings during the Second World War.

terrorism (noun)

Violent actions intended to frighten a large number of people to achieve a political goal.

Some groups try to achieve their political ideals through acts of terrorism.

genocide (noun)

The deliberate killing of people who belong to a specific group, be it religious, by race, etc.

The death of thousands of innocent people among ethnic groups in the area is now being recognized as genocide.

famine (noun)

When there is not enough food for a population, leading to mass starvation and public distress.

The ongoing conflict has not only brought devastation, but also widespread famine to the region.

guerrilla (noun)

Armed forces that are not part of a country's military, which employ unsanctioned tactics and frequently engage in illegal activities to achieve their own goals.

The guerrilla declared themselves "saviours" who are forced to fight for our freedom.

casualty (noun)

A person killed in an armed conflict, usually refers to civilian deaths.

The number of casualties the bombings have caused is staggering.

invasion (noun)

The act of a country, unfriendly army, or group, arriving in an area or region sometimes with aggressive intent and usually unwanted by those already there.

The conflict began a month ago after an invasion of enemy troops in the capital.

occupation (noun)

A period of time when a place is taken over by armed forces.

After a short period of occupation, the armed forces withdrew when the peace treaty was ratified.

siege (noun)

A prolonged conflict in a specific place by surrounding it and attacking with armed forces.

The siege lasted for weeks before the enemy finally surrendered their position.

1 **Put the following words into groups according to whether you think they are related to conflict, mediation, or peace:**

hostility   offensive   escalation
arbitration   negotiation   force
compromise   peacebuilding   insurgency
conflict resolution   decommissioning of arms   reconciliation
guerrilla warfare   conciliation   disarmament
pacifism   civil disobedience   coup d'état
non-violence   compromise   concession
intervention   concession
diplomacy   demilitarization

conflict	mediation	peace
hostility		

2 **Put each group of phrases in order, starting from 'strongly disagreeing' to 'agreement'. (The first phrase in each question is given as a starting point for you.)**

i)   get to an agreement / think through / see your point / run up against

run up against ➜ _____ ➜ _____ ➜ _____

ii) couldn't agree more / turn against / bring around / win around

turn against ➜ _____ ➜ _____ ➜ _____

iii) side with / believe in / out of the question / fall in with

out of the question ➜ _____ ➜ _____ ➜ _____

3 **Listen to the first episode of this podcast. Then discuss your thoughts on it with a classmate.**

Peace and Conflict – Understanding Our World
From Queen's University Belfast.

4   **Watch this Ted Talk. Then discuss and share your opinions.**

Peace Building Starts Small
Speaker: Claudia Meier
TEDxBern

5   **Read these quotes about peace and conflict. Share, think about, and discuss these quotes with your classmates.**

Diversity is an aspect of human existence that cannot be eradicated by terrorism or war or self-consuming hatred. It can only be conquered by recognizing and claiming the wealth of values it represents for all.

Splendid Literarium: A Treasury of Stories, Aphorisms, Poems, and Essays

Aberjhani, American historian

Beneath the armour of skin/and/bone/and/mind most of our colours are amazingly the same.

Elemental: The Power of Illuminated Love

Aberjhani, American historian

equality (noun)

The state of being equal. In society, we use it to describe a situation where members of a community, group, or family all have the same status, responsibilities, and rights, irrespective of race, gender, religion, age, etc.

We often talk about equality in society, but I feel most strongly about age discrimination and making sure young people have a voice which is heard.

inequality (noun)

The state of being unequal. In society, where there are significant differences in the situation for members of a community, group, or family, particularly in relation to wealth, access to education, healthcare, and other opportunities.

There is thought to be a strong link between economic inequality and poor health outcomes.

equity (noun)

The act of being treated fairly and be given the same opportunities.

We should strive for equity and fair opportunities for all.

inequity (noun)

The act of being treated unfairly, while not being awarded equal opportunity.

The fight against inequity and unfair treatment begins with the education we give our children at home.

parity (noun)

The act of being treated equally, especially in matters of compensation and position in a workplace.

Cries for parity in wages has been one of the strongest demands from the feminist movement.

diversity (noun)

1 A wide range and variety of people, cultures, ideas, etc.

Humans are not necessarily the same, that is why diversity is something to be celebrated and respected. Let our differences help us grow, not divide us.

2 The inclusion of a wide range of cultures, genders, races etc in a place, group or organization.

The school received an award for promoting and celebrating diversity in education.

acceptance (noun)

Including others without reservation or hesitation.

The acceptance of other cultures and beliefs should be our first instinct, not rejection.

social exclusion (noun)

A situation where certain groups or individuals feel isolated from society or are made to feel separate from conventional society.

Lockdown during the COVID-19 pandemic, whilst it was intended to keep them safe, frequently made many old people feel abandoned, alone, and victims of social exclusion.

to be (well-) represented/ underrepresented (verb)

Where people from a certain group or area are sufficiently present in a place or involved in an activity, we say they are well-represented. If they are underrepresented, there are not enough of them.

Despite the fact that the youth represent at least 20% of a country's population, they are noticeably underrepresented in parliaments. For example, people aged 18–35 are underrepresented in the European Parliament at 11%.

fairness (noun)

The notion of something being reasonable or acceptable for all people.

In an effort to promote fairness for all, the government amended some old, outdated laws.

just (adj)

Something that is completely fair, reasonable, or deserving.

Ten years imprisonment was a just sentence for such a terrible crime.

egalitarian (adj)

The belief that no person is more important than another and everyone is entitled to the same opportunities and rights in their lives.

Becoming a more egalitarian society takes effort and good intentions from all of us.

empowerment (noun)

The ability to do what you want and be in control of your own fate.

In recent years, those living with a disability have achieved more prominent roles in politics; a clear sign of empowerment that should not lose momentum.

solidarity (noun)

A show of support for other people or members of a group, often in a political situation.

As a sign of solidarity, the leaders shook hands and exchanged gifts at the start of the meeting.

dignity (noun)

Respect for the importance and value of a person.

All people must be treated with dignity, no matter their race or status in life.

validation (noun)
A feeling that focuses on being accepted by others.
She felt a sense of validation and pride when she became the first female CEO the company had ever had.

feminism (noun)
A movement that believes women should be treated fairly and equally and given the same amount of opportunities, recognitions, rights, etc, as men.
Feminism focuses on fair and equitable treatment for women everywhere, not the subjugation of men.

matriarchy (noun)
A society where women are in control or hold the power as leaders.
The Minangkabau people of West Sumatra, Indonesia, are known as a matriarchy. Laws require all property is passed down from mother to daughter, and they also believe the mother to be the most important person in society.

patriarchy (noun)
A society where men are in control or hold the power as leaders.
Some people still consider modern days societies as patriarchies, due to their outdated, sexist laws and customs.

sexism (noun)
The belief, behaviour and attitude of people who believe that one sex is inferior to the other, usually referring to sexism against females.
Sexism in the workplace should not be tolerated but sadly it still exists.

individuality (noun)
What makes someone unique, different from others.
Our style of clothing and the way we interact with others, among other things, are some of the ways we express our individuality.

emancipation (noun)
The process of giving a particular group of people political freedom and rights.
The emancipation of women in developing countries means that more women can go to work and have careers.

dominance (noun)
The more important, prevalent, stronger, etc, thing in a particular context or circumstance.
Through dominance by a majority, minorities can be discriminated against and even segregated from everyone else.

impartiality (noun)
Not supporting any side in an argument.
The Red Cross and Red Crescent societies are guided by the principle of Impartiality; they work to alleviate suffering of all, dependent on need and not in relation to nationality, race, religious belief, or political opinion.

partisan (adj)
Describes someone who strongly supports a side/team, cause, or political party, sometimes with strong emotion and without careful reflection or consideration of their actions.
Whilst the referee must always be impartial and unbiased, the noise of the partisan crowds may influence decisions.

biased (adj)
Describes someone who is more in favour of one opinion, side/team, activity, or cause than another.
If I'm honest, I feel as if he is quite biased against women.

distribution of wealth (noun)
Where the money, property, or other valuable things amongst members of a group or country is shared out, sometimes unfairly.
Is there increasing inequality in the world because there is an unfair distribution of wealth?

gap between rich and poor (phrase)
The difference between those with the most money, property, and valuable things and those who have very few of these.
Economic inequality is often measured by the gap between rich and poor.

financial independence (noun)
Where someone does not need to rely on someone else for money but earns enough from work to pay for everyday living expenses.
When I got my first job, I was on that first step to financial independence from my parents.

to live with a disability (verb, phrase)
Where an illness, injury, or mental or physical condition restricts someone or means they face additional challenges in their daily activities.
One in four people in the US live with some sort of disability, but they are underrepresented in government.

1 **Match words from the box on the right with words on the left to create phrases. Think about and discuss these phrases with your classmates. (The first one has been started for you.)**

i) contentious

   contentious issues

ii) male

   _____

iii) quality

   _____

iv) women´s

   _____

v) domestic

   _____

vi) gender

   _____

vii) gender pay

   _____

viii) inclusive

   _____

dominance
equality
empowerment
work
education
gap
issues
education

2 **Look at these groups of words. Find the odd one out in each group.**

   i) unfairness   evenness   sameness
   ii) inequality   inequity   fairness
   iii) masculinity   femininity   patriarchy
   iv) unlikeliness   unreasonableness   unfairness

3 **Watch this Ted Talk. Then discuss and share your opinions with your classmates.**

We should all be feminist
Chimamanda Ngozi Adichie, December 2012
https://www.ted.com/talks/chimamanda_ngozi_adichie_we_should_all_be_feminists

E Globalization

to globalize (verb)
To become known or to be present all around the world.
In an effort to globalize their brand, they decided to launch a new product in international markets.

industrialization (noun)
Growth of production and manufacturing industries.
Rapid industrialization can make other sectors of the economy suffer under the swift transition.

trade (noun)
The buying and selling of goods between individuals or countries.
During the COVID-19 pandemic, international trade took a very hard blow.

fair trade (noun)
A global movement that works directly with farmers and growers and their customers to ensure they are paid a reasonable price for their produce.
They were able to purchase a tractor, thanks to the extra revenue earned from the crops since they'd been working with new customers through fair trade.

global supply chain (noun)
The networks which ensure that goods and services are available all around the world.
It's essential that we use the global supply chain effectively to ensure the availability of the COVID-19 vaccine in all parts of the world.

tariff (noun)
A fee or charge to do something, often associated with importing and exporting.
Some countries decided to export less when the tariffs increased.

free movement of goods (noun)
When companies or countries trade with each other and there are no tariffs or fees involved.
It was easy to expand into other places thanks to the free movement of goods.

trade bloc (noun)
When a particular group of countries agree on a special set of terms of trade with each other, that other countries are not eligible for.
It can be difficult to trade with a country if they are already part of a trade bloc with other countries.

trade agreement (noun)
When two or more countries set the terms for trade to take place between them.
The trade agreement meant that export tariffs on foods were reduced, which helped farmers greatly as they were able to sell more crops to foreign markets.

to import (verb)
To purchase goods from international markets.
We import goods that we can't manufacture ourselves from a neighbouring country.

to export (verb)
To sell goods to international markets.
We have a surplus of grain each year which we export to other countries.

to exchange (verb)
To give something and receive something in return.
International trade is essentially the exchange of goods and services between countries for an agreed price.

interdependence (noun)
When one country, area or state relies heavily on another.
Most states in a region share a high level of economic interdependence with one another.

interconnected (adj)
Something that is in contact with many other things in many different ways.
The world is more interconnected than ever thanks to globalization.

financial (adj)
In relation to money and its management.
Global financial markets have also been strongly affected by the pandemic.

debt (noun)
Money that is owed.
National debt reached an all-time high after the war ended.

loan (noun)
Borrowed money that needs to be paid back in an agreed amount of time, usually with interest.
Loans are frequently issued to developing countries, in hopes of future profitable investments.

tax (noun)
Money that people pay to the government, usually paid directly from a person's salary or attached to fees from services, properties, actions, etc, destined for public use.
One of the cornerstones of any economic system are taxes.

investment (noun)
Money that is put into something with the hope of making a profit or gaining an advantage.
Some investments can be a gamble if you don't understand how the market works.

growth (noun)
Increased production and capabilities of an economy or business.
Some countries have seen significant growth due to foreign investment.

consumerism (noun)
Increased focus and attention to buying and having products.
We must make a conscious effort to shy away from consumerism and waste if we hope to keep our planet safe.

developed (adj)
A more advanced area or thing.
Developed countries tend to employ more people in the service sector than in agriculture.

developing (adj)
On the path to becoming a stronger, more advanced thing.
Developing economies face hard challenges when political instability becomes a constant issue.

multinational (adj)
Operating in several different countries.
Some multinational companies share integrated practices throughout all of their branches around the world.

cosmopolitan (adj)
Having a variety of people, experiences, cultures, etc, from diverse places of the world.
Port cities are usually the most cosmopolitan in a country, due to increased international trade and merging of different cultures that come with it.

to outsource (verb)
To pay another company or individual to do a particular aspect of a company's work.
Large companies tend to outsource some of their jobs, like packaging, to smaller local companies to cut costs.

logistics (noun)
The organization of many different aspects or components to enable a process to be carried out as effectively as possible.
Handling logistics for a multinational organization is challenging when global trade can be easily disrupted by natural disasters such as earthquakes or a pandemic.

competitiveness (noun)
The process of having the ability to successfully compete with other countries, organizations, etc.
Some countries have a heightened sense of competitiveness when it comes to international sports events.

1 Complete these phrases using one of these words:

capital   barriers   interdependence   cultural   supply   borders

i)   open/close/respect _____

ii)   mobility of goods, _____, and people

iii)   _____ and economic ties

iv)   good side/dark side of _____

v)   erect/demolish _____

vi)   _____ chain problems

2 Reorder these words to make quotations about globalization. Think about the meanings of the quotes and discuss your ideas with a partner.

i)   of / in / the / we / often / indifference / globalization / too / participate

        Pope Francis

ii)   economic / to / it / that / out / is / the / globalization / entire / negative / wipes / side / systems

        Peter Berger

iii)   our / some / from / other / to / of / and / at / we / globalization / countries / ideas / means / re-examine / have / look / ideas

        Herbie Hancock

3 Explore and enjoy. Share, discuss, and think about these articles with your classmates:

Globalisation in the time of COVID-19: repositioning Africa to meet the immediate and remote challenges
By Sanni Yaya, Akaninyene Otu and Ronald Labonté
BMC, 24th June 2020

THE IMPACT OF COVID-19 ON GLOBALIZATION
By Nistha Shrestha and Ubydul Haque et al
Science Direct, 20th December 2020

F Ethics

individualism (noun)
Belief that the interests of the individual are the most important.
In some societies, people hold such a strong sense of individualism, that it clashes with their inherent desire for cooperation.

collective (adj)
Shared responsibilities, feelings, etc.
Moral laws are formed through a collective desire to live in harmony.

collective (noun)
A community or business set up for each worker/member to have an equal share of the profits.
The shop is actually a collective; it was started ten years ago by local villagers.

idealism (noun)
Believing you can achieve your ideals, even if it is perceived as unlikely by others.
Even after all his failings, his idealism holds him strong and willing to try as many times as needed.

faith (noun)
Deep trust in something or someone.
I have great faith in my neighbours. It might be slightly idealistic to think that we can fix our community, but I know we can do it!

altruism (noun)
Be willing to help others, even at your own expense and not expect anything in return.
In a great show of altruism, he donated most of his clothes to the needy, stating that he had enough to be alright.

dogma (noun)
A belief that is expected to be accepted without question.
Some religious dogmas should be viewed a little more critically, lest they harm others in an effort to stay pious.

rectitude (noun)
To be morally correct in judgement and action.
She defended her friends despite not being involved, showing rectitude and great responsibility, for she knew they were innocent.

exemplar (noun)
An ideal example.
She was considered the exemplar of dedication, after she graduated with honours and went to become a very successful businesswoman.

moderation (noun)
When something is done within sensible limits.
Doing everything in moderation ensures a healthy balance and avoids addictions.

stoicism (noun)
The act of enduring pain or hardship without showing emotion.
Through sheer stoicism, he stood there doing his job as a fireman, despite knowing his friend had passed away in the explosion.

humility (noun)
Not showing excessive pride because you are aware of your flaws and shortcomings.
Through an act of great humility, she stepped down from the podium and placed her first-place medal on the other competitor who had lost because of an accidental mistake.

to moralize (verb)
To make judgements based on what is right or wrong.
Some people feel the need to moralize every single action others make, without looking inwards at their own behaviour.

immoral (adj)
Outside of society's expected moral behaviour, to act morally wrong.
His immoral actions got him demoted from his position in the disciplinary committee.

amoral (adj)
Having no morals at all.
Animals are amoral, they act on instinct, not on expected behaviour.

moral dilemma (noun)
A dilemma is a situation where you are presented with two (or possibly more) options and have to make a difficult decision between them. A moral dilemma is where you have to choose between options based on what you believe is right or wrong.
Should we give animals rights, even if that means humans suffer? That's a moral dilemma many scientists face.

to cross a (or the) line (verb)
To begin to behave in an inappropriate or immoral way.
His jokes are usually very funny, but I think sometimes he crosses a line, and makes a joke which some people find unacceptable.

ethos (noun)

Set of beliefs and traits relating to the social interactions of a person or group.

Their religion's ethos focuses on caring for others and treating people fairly.

pathos (noun)

The power to make you feel sadness or sympathy.

As a literary device, pathos ensures that the reader develops a strong emotional connection to the narrative.

euthanasia (noun)

The act of killing someone who is ill and unlikely to get better. In this way death is seen as ending their suffering. In some countries and cultures, this is illegal. (See **assisted suicide**.)

I just cannot see how anyone could argue in favour of euthanasia. To me, it is morally unacceptable.

assisted suicide (noun)

The act of killing yourself with the help of someone else, possibly a doctor/physician, when you are ill and unlikely to get better.

Physician assisted suicide has been legal in the whole of Canada since 2016.

to disagree on religious grounds (verb)

Where two individuals or groups of people cannot agree because of religious reasons, i.e. where each is of a religion which lays down a different code of behaviour or set of morals or values.

The doctor and the patient's family couldn't decide the best course of action because they disagreed on religious grounds.

genetic modification (noun)

The activity in modern science of placing a gene from one organism into another in order to improve a certain characteristic. Also called genetic engineering.

I believe that genetic modification is morally wrong. It is not ethical to create new life forms in this way.

1 Sort the following words according to whether you think they have positive or negative connotations.

nepotism   moral   virtue   honesty   value   violate   honour

moral   immoral   corrupt   decent   genteel   ethos   opportunist   greedy

Positive connotation	Negative connotation

2 Use the following words to complete the quotations. After completing them take a minute to reflect upon their meaning.

beast   difference   principles   ethics   man

have   what   world   calendar

i) _____ and equity and the _____ of justice do not change with the _____

    D H Lawrence

ii) A _____ without ethics is a wild _____ loosed upon this _____

    Albert Camus

iii) Ethics is knowing the _____ between _____ you _____ the right to do
     and what is right to do.

    Potter Stewart

3 Watch this Ted Talk. Then discuss and share your opinions with your classmates.

Ethics, yes even when nobody is watching
Dawn Ware, October 2019
https://www.ted.com/talks/dawne_ware_ethics_yes_even_when_nobody_is_watching

urban (adj)
In relation to towns and/or cities.
Urban development planning takes careful consideration of the possible effects on the environment.

urbanism (noun)
The character of life in cities and the study of what is needed in urban societies.
Through the great feats of urbanism, some have the luxury of living in great sprawling cities with many amenities and safety.

urbanized (adj)
To include all the components of an urban area, such as buildings, factories, offices, etc.
Urbanized regions of the country have reported power outages due to the terrible storm.

suburb (noun)
Residential area on the edge of a city or large town.
Many people envy those living in the suburbs since they have easier access to open spaces and can often work from home.

infrastructure (noun)
All the components and systems that allow a city to function, such as transport, power supply, etc.
A city's infrastructure is dependent on the proper management and maintenance of its services.

transport (or transportation) network (noun)
A system made up of roads, train tracks, and services such as airplanes, ferries, etc. for the movement of people or goods.
One of the best things about living in a big city is the excellent transport networks.

to rely on public transport (or transportation) (verb)
To depend on and make significant use of the network of buses, trains, trams, metro, etc.
Many young people living in rural areas have to rely on public transport to meet friends until they learn to drive.

rush-hour traffic (noun, idiom)
Increased number of vehicles on the roads at peak (busy) times of day when people are travelling to or from their place of work.
If we don't leave early enough, we'll get caught in the rush-hour traffic.

traffic jam (noun)
When vehicles on the road come to a standstill or are moving very slowly.
He was late for work and missed the meeting because he'd been stuck in a traffic jam.

pedestrianized (adj)
An area or zone where vehicles of any kind are not permitted.
Many streets in the centre of town are now pedestrianized in an effort to improve air quality and reduce pollution.

municipality (noun)
A self-governed city or town.
The municipality was completely against the new national laws proposed by the government and decided not to implement them.

inhabitant (noun)
A person that resides in a particular place.
The inhabitants of the municipality were in favour of the new national laws proposed by the local government.

neighbour (noun)
A person that lives close by.
Many British people feel that the pandemic made their relationships with their neighbours much stronger.

neighbourhood (noun)
Different residential areas surrounding one's home, with distinct characteristics.
Our neighbourhood has become safer since the municipality increased security operations in the area.

metropolitan (adj)
In relation to a large city.
The metropolitan area has seen plenty of growth after the influx of resources from international investors.

inner-city (adj)
The oldest and usually poorest central area of a city.
Efforts are being made to restore the inner-city to some semblance of its former glory.

poverty (noun)
Extremely lacking in money and possessions, being in the poorest state possible.
Many rural communities are in danger of suffering from extreme poverty if government investment doesn't start soon.

rural (adj)

In relation to the countryside and more modest living, away from large cities.

Rural areas all share a wonderful rustic feel that give them their charming aspect.

rural exodus (noun)

The departure of (mostly) young people from the countryside to find jobs and homes in towns and cities.

The rural exodus is making it increasingly difficult for rural farmers to find reliable labourers for tasks such as harvesting.

teleworking (noun)

Working from home and making use of the telephone, a computer, virtual meeting software, etc. rather than meeting people face-to-face.

Teleworking became so common during the pandemic that many people now understand that they can live further away from their work and only go into the office a few days each week.

second home (noun)

An additional house often for use on the weekend or for holidays, usually in the countryside or by the sea.

Sadly, the increasing number of second homes in coastal areas has pushed up the price of housing for local people.

rustic (adj)

Having a simple and rough appearance, very characteristic of a rural environment.

Her rustic farmhouse in the countryside is a lovely getaway from the busy streets of the metropolitan area.

countryside (noun)

A large area of land that is used for farming or left as it is naturally.

The countryside is teeming with wildlife and beautiful sights.

townspeople (noun)

Residents from a particular town.

The townspeople were appalled by the new taxes imposed on them.

agriculture (noun)

The work of farming.

Most of the ancient world depended on agriculture as their primary means of subsistence.

agrarian (adj)

Relating to farmers, farming and that way of life.

Her agrarian lifestyle ensured that she lived her final years in relative peace and tranquillity in the countryside.

farmland (noun)

Land used to rear animals or grow crops.

They still had plenty of farmland that was not being used, so they decided to diversify and use a field as a campsite.

commercial crops (noun)

Plants that are grown and harvested in large amounts on farms to sell for profits.

Commercial crops can be a great source of income for farmers.

subsistence crops (noun)

Small amounts of plants that are grown and harvested by a farmer and are used to feed themselves and their families.

Families in many developing countries rely on subsistence crops as a means of survival.

pastoral (adj)

Something that is typical of traditional countryside life and/or landscapes.

Many people enjoy living in rural areas because of the beautiful pastoral views.

outback (noun)

A very isolated rural area, usually in reference to large desert regions of Australia.

Resources are hard to come by in the outback during dry seasons.

remote (adj)

Very far away.

The remote, outlying settlements seem very alien to the inhabitants of the inner-city.

idyllic (adj)

Extremely beautiful and tranquil.

This idyllic countryside is the result of many years of preservation and protection of these spaces.

1 **Find the odd one out in each group of words.**

   i) cosmopolitan, metropolitan, suburban

   ii) bustling, sparse, village

   iii) picturesque, charming, decayed

   iv) townsfolk, megapolis, hometown

   v) infrastructure, amenities, sprawling

2 **These idioms and phrases all relate to the urban and rural environment. Use the words below to complete the idioms and phrases. (Use each word only once.)**

   nowhere   hive   ivory   chaff   water   street

   i) Live in an _____ tower.

   ii) Separate the wheat from the _____

   iii) In the middle of _____

   iv) A _____ of activity.

   v) That's _____ under the bridge.

   vi) The man in the _____

3 **Read the following proverb and quote. Think about their meanings and then discuss them with your classmates.**

   "A great city, a great solitude."

   Proverb

   "Our admiration of the antique is not admiration of the old, but of the natural."

   R W Emerson

4 **Listen to this radio report in which people discuss similarities between urban and rural communities. Make notes about the similarities and differences people mention then share your opinions with your classmates. You can listen to the report and read a transcript on the NPR website.**

   Urban And Rural Americans Have More In Common Than They Might Think
   NPR website (npr.org)
   12th November 2020

Language for the oral assessment

A Describing a photo or image (SL)

There are plenty of words we may use to describe a picture and its components. To help you in your descriptions for the oral assessment, remember that:

- Descriptions must make good use of all your senses to ensure you don't miss anything. So think about what you *see* and also what you *feel* when looking at the image.
- Images are metaphors; they show somebody's point of view. This means that an image may often go beyond the initial superficial meaning, and end up showing more than what is visually presented at first glance.

Here are some examples of words and phrases that will help you describe any photo or image perfectly.

First/general impressions of the photo/image

It's a photo about …	At first glance, it looks like …
Your attention is immediately drawn to …	I saw/observed/noticed straightaway the …
The picture deals with the theme of …	The photo/drawing/image is possibly about the topic …
The general impression we get here is that …	This drawing clearly illustrates …
What I see first in the picture is/are …	First of all, I saw the … in the image
This illustration indicates the theme of …	It's landscape format (*ie it's longer along the top and bottom than the sides*)
This photo suggests the photographer is …	It's portrait format (*ie it's longer along the sides than the top and bottom*)
The scene takes place in/at …	In the photo, you can see/make out …
It looks like the photo was taken …	I imagine this photo dates from …

In this picture, we can see a lion looking towards the sky.

The picture clearly shows a crocodile stalking his prey, waiting for the perfect moment to strike.

There are a couple of children playing with a bunch of toys, in what seems to be a very large playground.

There are some people walking around the plaza, being looked at by a group of tourists from a tour bus, almost as if they were looking at animals in a safari. I can deduce this from the expressions on their faces and how many of them are taking pictures.

Describing the picture in more detail

Position

In front of/at the front of the image/in the foreground	Between the …
Behind the …/at the back of the picture/in the background	Half-way down, I can see …
On the left of …/on the left-hand side	In the bottom right/bottom left, there is a …
On the right of …/on the right-hand side	In the top right/top left, there is a …
On the top half …/in the top part …/on top of …	Opposite the …
In the upper part …	Next to the …
Underneath the…/under the …/below the …	Between the …
In the lower part …/in the lower half …	On closer analysis, you can see …
In the upper part …/in the upper half …	A more detailed look makes me think that
In the middle of the image …	Assessing it in more detail/a more thorough assessment …

I can see that in front of the store, the woman appears to be waiting for someone.

Behind the dumpster, there appears to be a couple of discarded shoes.

On the left-hand side, there is a bright blue balloon flying away from the hands of a little girl.

While on the right-hand side, there's a pony with some colourful ribbons eating some hay, showing the peaceful atmosphere of life in the countryside.

On top of the fridge, there are a bunch of old magazines covered in dust.

In the lower part of the picture, the sea seems calm and inviting.

While in the upper part of the picture, the sky seems menacing, as if a storm is coming!

Between the trees, there are a couple of foxes chasing a rabbit, which in my opinion links to sharing the planet and how people who are perceived as 'weak' get chased off.

What the photo/image depicts

This picture depicts …	It seems (to me) that …
The photographer is trying to communicate/show us that …	This picture/scene/illustration seems to show …
It looks like …	I guess that the …
This photo could be a metaphor for …	This picture speaks to me because …
This reminds me of …/I'm reminded of …	What I find interesting/surprising/shocking is …
I think it's/I don't think it's …	

In the background of the picture, there is a beautiful sunset that makes the sky look like it's on fire!

While in the foreground, there is a beautiful beach full of people who seem to be having a good time. I'm reminded of the 'leisure activities' sub-theme and how everyone gets along nicely.

Next to the old woman, there's a cute little dog with a bright pink collar, apparently trying to jump on her lap as she sits. This reminds me of how humans instil some of their identity into their pets, as an extension of their own personality.

Making cultural links

It seems clear that this photo is taken in …	I think this is taken in … owing to the fact that/because of …
I would suggest that this image takes place in …	The … we can see indicates that this is in …
In my opinion, this is typically American.	From what I know/have read/have experienced/have seen, this illustrates a custom …
I would definitely guess that this is a typical scene in …	Like/similar to/parallel to/comparable to …
This shows a celebration/custom/tradition that is typically English … because we can see …	Unlike/in contrast to/contrary to/different to …

1 Match words from each column to make phrases you can use to refer to the exact location of something in a photo/image that you want to describe. You can use the same words more than once.

on		left-hand side
		right-hand side
		lower part
	(the) front of	upper part
in		top
	the	bottom
		foreground
at		background
		middle/centre

2 Complete these sentence starters with these words. You can use the words more than once.

inspires   shows   illustrates   depicts   personifies
looks as   criticizes   poses   makes me think   inspires me
expresses   communicates   looks/seems like   relates to

i)   The illustration _____

ii)   The artist _____

iii) The highlighted message _____

iv)   The global issue _____

v)   The picture _____

vi)   The photographer _____

vii) The aim of the picture _____

viii) The main focus of the picture _____

3 Choose from the words below to complete these phrases which you can use to give your opinion about a photo/image. You can use the words more than once.

frighteningly   portrayal   message   moment   slightly   outstanding
image   unexpectedly   vividly   openly   clearly   scene

i)   _____ alarming

ii)   captivating _____

iii) impressive _____

iv)   evocative _____

v)   _____ unrealistic

vi)   _____ ingenious

vii) _____ impersonal

viii) _____ moving

ix)   _____ humorous

x)   pleasant _____

4 Think about the following quotation. Discuss it with your classmates and share your opinions on it.

> Taking an image, freezing a moment, reveals how rich reality truly is.
>
> *Anonymous*

B Describing a literary extract (HL)

Referring to the extract	
It's an extract/poem/letter about …	This must be/is likely to be a poem/extract/article from/by …
On first reading through/My first thought was …	The language/dialect/idioms is/are used by the author to …
It seems to show/is on the theme of/refers to/alludes to/deals with the issue of …	The scene/monologue/lecture/speech takes place in/at …

Referring to characters/facts/topics	
In my opinion, …/I am convinced that …/I am confident this …	As a keen reader of novels/newspapers/blogs, I think …
As far as I understand, from what is being discussed/described, …/I am persuaded that …	This scene/conversation/dialogue/narrative/poem reminds me of …/appears to show …
The main character/protagonist/narrator/author/writer is showing the reader …	We know it takes place in … because of the topic/voices/accent/informal tone.
The … symbolizes/illustrates/characterizes …	The author creates an atmosphere of …
The extract inspires me/excites me/interests me because of …	This is a satire/criticism/illustration of today's society/the political situation of the last decade.
The poem makes me think of …/leaves me feeling scared/makes me laugh out loud.	The message/mood/atmosphere/comedy of the extract is …

Using quotations	
For example, the main character says '…'	I have to disagree most strongly with the writer in the first/last phrase, because …
I could quote this part of the poem …	The part which refers to … made me laugh/cry/want to shout out.
To use an example taken from this extract …	To quote the author '…' end quote.
I could paraphrase this extract by saying …	As the writer states in the opening/closing lines …
I would heartily agree with the writer when he/she says …	By using the word/phrase/expression …, the author is describing/relating/telling …

Making links to the culture	
It seems clear that this extract was written by an English/Australian/American author ….	I would definitely guess that this describes a typical Canadian/western/modern-day activity.
This story/act/conversation is likely to take place in the UK/the US/Canada/North America, because …	This refers to a celebration/custom/tradition/festival that is typical of …
I would suggest that this scene takes place in …	According to the customs/traditions/conventions of this country, this …
In my opinion, this is a typically American extract.	I'm not sure where this takes place, since it is so different to my culture/any culture I have experienced, because …

1 These words are all related to literature. Put the following words into the correct group.

tragedy   comedy   symbolism   characterization   colloquialism   fiction
conflict   scene   emotive language   fiction   imagery   metaphor   mood
atmosphere   protagonist   idioms   poetry   non-fiction   dialect
monologue   plot   satire   tone

Genre	Literary devices	Literary elements	Use of language

2 Choose from the words below to create alternative phrases which you can use to discuss literature. You can use the words more than once.

enumerates   recollects   reflects   contrasts   validates   discloses
explodes   praises   enunciates   justifies   begs   urges
praises   distinguishes   contrasts   interrogates

i)   The text connotes/manifests/emphasizes/_____/_____/_____.

ii)   The character confesses/reveals/_____/_____/_____.

iii)   The writer states/claims/depicts/_____/_____/_____.

iv)   The narrator lectures/echoes/_____/_____/_____.

v)   The reader infers/links/_____/_____.

3 Match words from each column to make phrases you can use to discuss literature. You can use the same words more than once.

	the	use (of)
the	the use of	rhetorical questions
by	persuasive	language
	using/including	of
through	repetition	suggests/implies/connotes
	chosen vocabulary	

4 Think about the following quotation. Discuss it with your classmates and share your opinions on it.

"Literature is where I go to explore the highest and lowest places in human society and in the human spirit, where I hope to find not absolute truth but the truth of the tale, of the imagination and of the heart."

A guide to text types

Here is a summary of the typical text types you will explore as part of your IB Diploma English B studies. This summary provides you with information such as:

- what the features of each text type are
- the intended purposes of them
- and the type of language they use.

Understanding these elements of different text types will enable you to produce work that is appropriate in a wide range of situations and contexts, and for a variety of audiences.

Note: It's important to remember that both the context and the audience should be presented to you beforehand either in the exam question or by your teacher, depending on the type of work you're asked to produce.

Text type	Text features
Article (newspaper, magazine)	• Must include a headline/title that should be engaging to the reader. • Main lead paragraph must include most of the relevant information to catch the reader's attention. • Focuses on facts and opinions to convey the information presented.
Blog	• Should focus on first-person narration of events. • Title should be catchy and interesting. • Should be engaging and relevant to the intended audience. • Use of common techniques such as rhetorical questions, invitations to comment, etc.
Brochure, leaflet, pamphlet	• Must include a title that should be engaging or interesting to the reader. • May include lists of features, bullet points, etc, to persuade the reader. • Should include various forms of contact information. • Usually, these texts include illustrations or elements of graphic design (although these are not evaluated in Paper 1).
Diary (private)/ journal	• Should focus on the first-person narration of events. • Makes use of emotion to express feelings and ideas about events. • Generally composed of various entries to string together a set of events in different temporal instances.
Informal email/ letter	• Will maintain focus on addressing a specific person or group. • Should have an appropriate greeting and send-off. • Should begin by contextualizing the topic of the email for the recipient. • Mostly intended to establish a friendly exchange between the participants.
Formal email/letter	• Will maintain a clear focus on addressing a specific person or group. • Should address the recipient by their formal title (eg Mr, Ms, Dr, etc) • Should have appropriate formal greetings and send-offs. • Should begin by contextualizing the topic of the email for the recipient.
Essay	• Should have an engaging title that is relevant to the argument to be presented. • Should include a clear introduction, stating the point to be addressed; a body detailing the elements of the topic and the arguments to be made; a proper conclusion that links all the elements presented in a clear closure.

Purpose	Language
Designed to inform the reader in an exploration of a particular topic. This could range from major events to restaurant recommendations.	Depending on the audience and context, the main goal is to inform the reader. So, the register should generally be formal or semi-formal. Easy to understand by the audience and engaging enough to keep them interested.
Blogs are mainly used to entertain, inform through experience, express opinions, etc. It's always important to remember that this could potentially be read by plenty of people interested in the topics and opinions you present.	Seeing as these are your own thoughts on the matters presented, language should mostly be semi-formal or informal. Blogs are intended to converse with others and get their feedback and opinions on what you're showing them.
Intended to inform or promote something. Usually organized in a way to catch the reader's attention and persuade them to engage in some form with the source.	Depending on the audience and context, the main goal is to inform the reader and persuade them. So the register should generally be formal or semi-formal. Text should be easy to understand by the audience and engaging enough to grab their attention and convince them of something, whether that is to buy, visit, support, etc.
Designed as an outlet to recollect and explain certain events through emotional descriptions and very personal opinions. Journals differ by the fact that they are usually more focused on a sort of 'log' of events and what occurred in them. They generally lean less on emotional components and more on descriptions. Journals might also be intended to be public, as opposed to diaries which are intended to be private.	Seeing as these are your own thoughts on the matters presented, language should mostly be semi-formal or informal. Focus on feelings and emotions, reacting to different events.
Intended to engage with the recipient. Expressing opinions, ideas, advice, etc.	Should generally use informal language, seeing as the recipient is a known acquaintance. Intended to converse and establish an exchange of opinions and thoughts.
Intended to engage with the recipient in a respectful manner. Presents a very specific statement, opinion, complaint, etc. Personal emotions should not be the focus. Focus should be placed on achieving the intended outcome of why the message is being written.	Should use formal language. Seeing as the recipient might not be known, or is in an important position, he/she must be addressed respectfully and in a serious manner.
This text type is intended to analyse, explore, or discuss a specific topic, using facts and well thought out argumentation.	The language used should be formal or semi-formal. The intended audience should be educated people who understand the presented information and are able to make sense of the presented arguments; therefore, the information should be presented in a coherent, logical, and well-organized manner.

Interview	• Must include a title that should be engaging or interesting to the reader.
	• May have a brief introduction to the reader about the person who is being interviewed.
	• Should use direct quotations from the participants.
	• Should involve various forms of questions, embedded into regular conversation.
News report	• Must include a headline/title that should be engaging to the reader.
	• Should be written in a neutral, impartial manner.
	• Focuses on facts rather than opinions.
Opinion column/ letter to the editor	• Must include a headline/title that should be engaging to the reader.
	• Main paragraph must include relevant information to catch the reader's attention.
	• Argumentative analysis and persuasive language are encouraged.
	• Facts and arguments should be presented.
Personal statement	• Must include a title that should be engaging to the reader.
	• Should include an engaging introduction, stating the point to be addressed, and a strong conclusion.
Proposal	• The title will usually carry with it the focus or intent of the proposal.
	• Points and objectives should be made clear from the beginning.
	• Information should be listed in the form of bullet points, intended to explore the steps needed to carry the proposal forward.
Report (official)	• Shares similarities with the letter format.
	• Should include:
	– a clear introduction stating the point to be addressed
	– a body detailing the elements of the report and their relevance
	– and a clear conclusion.
Review	• Should include the author's name.
	• Title should be catchy and interesting.
	• Should be engaging and relevant to the intended audience.
	• Facts and arguments should be presented.
Set of instructions, guidelines	• The title will usually carry with it the focus or intent of the proposed guidelines.
	• Point and objectives should be made clear from the beginning.
	• Information should be listed in the form of bullet points, and explore the steps needed to achieve the intended outcome.
Speech, presentation, debate	• Information should be accompanied by strong, compelling statements.
	• Beginning should have a strong impact, while the ending should leave a lasting impression.
	• Strong use of literary devices and persuasive techniques is highly encouraged.

Mostly, interviews are used to inform, report, explore, debate, etc, but it all depends on the context and the participants. As opposed to a questionnaire that simply focuses on questions and answers, interviews tend to focus on getting a response through conversation and dialogue between the participants. The interviewer uses various types of questions and techniques, to involve the interviewed person and ensure a meaningful exchange.	The language used should be formal or semi-formal. Through conversation, the participants should explore different topics and give their opinions on the matter.
Designed to inform the reader in a fact-based exploration of a particular topic. Focus is placed on specific events to be explored objectively.	Depending on the audience and context, the main goal is to inform the reader. So, the register should generally be formal or semi-formal, easy to understand by the audience, and engaging enough to keep them interested and well-informed.
This text type is mostly designed to inform and explore a particular topic in the form of an opinion, through argumentation and thought-provoking language. Therefore, the initial statement should act in response to a particular topic or previous work by someone else. Keep in mind that while both the opinion column and the letter to the editor share a similar purpose, the opinion column is written by a professional journalist while the letter may be written by a regular person.	The language used should be formal or semi-formal. Through argumentation, the writer should explore the topic and give his/her opinions on the matter.
Mostly intended to convey a clear set of events that engage the reader and let the author be understood. Remember that this is mostly used in instances such as college applications, which is why persuasive elements should be present as well.	Language should mostly be semi-formal, considering the objective is to convey personal events in an engaging, inviting manner. Information should be easy to understand by the audience and engaging enough to grab their attention.
It's quite important to remember that you're not only proposing a new idea or method, but you should also detail the steps to be taken, pros and cons, etc. For this, you should make good use of persuasive techniques and present your information in a coherent logical order.	The language used should be formal or semi-formal. Through persuasive and argumentative techniques, the writer should explore the topic and convincingly express ideas and position on different elements and why they're relevant to the overall proposal.
The overall purpose of this text type is to provide a detailed account of events as objectively as possible.	Should use formal language. The events must be detailed in a serious manner. Descriptive writing techniques should be used.
Intended to judge a particular piece of work, present information, and explore the finer points that constitute the piece being judged/reviewed.	The language used should be formal or semi-formal. Through argumentation, the writer should explore the piece and give his opinions on the matter, detailing and exploring its components.
Mostly intended to ensure certain behaviour or protocol is followed in specific situations.	The language used should be formal or semi-formal. Intended to convey clear, very specific or general instructions/guidelines.
With these three text types, the objective is not only to inform but mainly to persuade the intended audience and for them to accept/follow your ideas. Therefore, information should be engaging, provocative and presented in an argumentative fashion. Literary devices and persuasive techniques are a must, along with the clever use of rhetorical questions.	The language used should be formal or semi-formal. Through persuasive and argumentative techniques, the writer should explore the topic and convincingly express his/her ideas and position on different elements, and why they should be relevant to the intended audience, with the intent to convince and inform them.

1 **Presenting an argument. The following steps characterize what you would do to present each part of an argument in an essay. Sort the steps into the correct group according to the part of the argument to which they relate.**

show the other side   state your view   identify the problem
identify the two sides of the argument   grab the reader's attention
end by communicating clearly your position   provide background information
present your position/view   recommend a course of action to the reader   explain the problem

	Body		
Introduction	**Paragraph 1**	**Paragraph 2**	**Conclusion**

2 **The following are useful connective words and phrases for written and oral work. Choose one of the words or phrases from the box to complete each line of connective words. (You could choose a word or phrase more than once.)**

in the case of   for this reason   likewise   so consequently   nevertheless
decidedly   despite   moreover   specifically

i)   **(for making comparisons)** equally/in comparison/similarly/ _____

ii)   **(to persuade)** evidently/clearly/surely/ _____

iii)   **(to show cause and effect)** hence/therefore/owing to/ _____

iv)   **(to contrast)** however/whereas/while/ _____

v)   **(to give an example)** such as/to show that/an instance/ _____

www.ingramcontent.com/pod-product-compliance
Lightning Source LLC
Chambersburg PA
CBHW050241221125
35745CB00031B/415